— SUPER GREEN —

Super Easy

Allen & Unwin
83 Alexander Street
Crows Nest NSW 2065
Australia
Phone: (61 2) 8425 0100
Email: info@allenandunwin.com
Web: www.allenandunwin.com

 A catalogue record for this
book is available from the
NATIONAL LIBRARY OF AUSTRALIA   National Library of Australia

ISBN 978 1 76011 080 2

CUP AND TABLESPOON MEASURES: We have used Australian cup measures,
of 250 ml (9 fl oz). Please note that the US and UK cup measures are slightly
smaller, approximately 235 ml (7¾ fl oz). We have also used 20 ml (4 teaspoon)
tablespoon measures. If you are using a 15 ml (3 teaspoon) tablespoon, add
an extra teaspoon of the ingredient for each tablespoon specified.

OVEN GUIDE: For fan-forced ovens, as a general rule, set the oven
temperature to 20°C (35°F) lower than indicated in the recipe.

Recipe photographs: Rob Palmer
Styling and props: David Morgan
Food preparation: Sarah Mayoh
Copy editor: Megan Johnston
Nutritional analysis: Chrissy Freer
Index: Puddingburn Publishing Services
Design: Sarah Odgers
Set in 8.5/11 pt Halcom Regular
Colour reproduction by Splitting Image Colour Studio Pty Ltd,
Clayton, Victoria
Printed and bound in China by C&C Offset Printing Co., Ltd
10 9 8 7 6 5 4 3 2 1

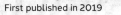

— SUPER GREEN —

Super Easy

Easy and **deliciously nourishing** recipes

SALLY OBERMEDER & MAHA CORBETT

ALLEN&UNWIN

SYDNEY·MELBOURNE·AUCKLAND·LONDON

Contents

Welcome

The beautiful thing about food is that it has the power to connect us all—there are few things more joyous in life than sharing a delicious meal with loved ones. For us, our favourite moments happen in the kitchen when family and friends have gathered to share stories, laugh together and make memories over meals that have been prepared and cooked with love.

What's also wonderful about cooking is that it is about connecting within—eating a nourishing meal is ultimately an act of self-care, which these days is more important than ever before, given the exhausting demands that are placed on us each and every day.

For so many of us, the days of working 9 to 5 have long gone. Now it can feel more like 24/7—and between work, family, friends, running households, social activities and more, it's no wonder so many people are fatigued and struggling to feel their best.

Day after day people share with us how tired they're feeling, how depleted their immunity is and how they're desperate to feel healthy, but they worry it's complicated, expensive or out of reach.

It's long been our mission to help change all that. We know from our own experience that feeling your absolute best can only start on the inside, with the fuel that you are putting into your body every day to nourish you and power you on.

We know that when you tackle food first and foremost, it gives you the energy you need to be able to manage the other demanding aspects of life.

We also know that when you're feeling good, it's addictive. People notice the difference in you, and they typically want in on the action. You notice the difference, too, because you feel leaner, you have more energy, you get more good quality sleep, your skin is softer and your immunity has improved. You're radiating good health and truly glowing from the inside out.

If you have followed our healthy lifestyle journey through our other cookbooks, on SWIISH.com or on our social media, you'll know that, when it comes to eating well, we love to share all we can, and to show you that it can be super easy, fast, lean and so incredibly delicious. We know that healthy food doesn't have to taste bland or boring, or leave you broke.

This book stays true to what we believe—that a predominantly plant-based lifestyle with added superfoods, good fats and oils, grains and lean protein is the way to go. In our recipes, we use plenty of shortcuts and staple ingredients in our fridges and pantries that maximise flavour and nutrition while saving you time and money.

We've divided *Super Easy* into six sections.

SALADS

Gone are the days when a salad was just some limp lettuce leaves drowned in a sugary store-bought dressing. Now, thanks to the wide variety of fresh veggies we are lucky enough to have access to, they're monster meals in themselves, filled with a rainbow of colour and taste. Our recipes, which include delicious dressings and flavour combos, will have you craving these salads daily.

ONE-POT MEALS

We get it, and we agree—there really aren't enough hours in the day. And there especially aren't enough hours to warrant washing up endless loads of dishes. These one-pot (or pan) meals save you precious time but still give you flavour-packed meals for all to enjoy.

BOWLS

This trend in food isn't going anywhere. The most Instagram-worthy of the lot, bowls are all about artfully arranged greens, grains, proteins and legumes—nutrient-rich and satisfying. We adore how they look and how they taste.

ONE-TRAY WONDERS

Say hello to the next big thing. One trays (also known as sheet pans—we will use the terms interchangeably in this book) are all about easy oven-based recipes. Literally, the entire meal—including the protein and veggies—is cooked on a flat baking tray in the oven. Set and forget, then simply enjoy! What could be better?

SMOOTHIES

Smoothies are a game changer. They're one of the fastest and easiest ways to get your greens and feel energised and lean. Smoothies give you the chance to significantly up your nutrient intake through a medley of leafy greens, good fats, veggies, superfoods and fruit. Smoothies make an excellent meal in general, and when you're pressed for time they're brilliant, as they're quick to make and easy to carry on the go.

SNACKS

Perfect for in-between meals, snacks are great for keeping you feeling full and satisfied. Some are raw, some are cooked, but they're all easy to prepare and many are perfect for school or office lunchboxes.

We truly hope that you cook the recipes in this book again and again, and feel your best and healthiest as a result.

For us, to play even a small role in helping you nurture the inside, and celebrate the outside, means everything.

Happy cooking!

Love, Sal & Maha xxx

Frequently asked questions

Do I need any special equipment to make the recipes in your book?

A handful of recipes call for a food processor but these are very inexpensive nowadays. You can even pick one up at a discount department store for under $50.

A blender is also a great kitchen essential that can be used for many different purposes—soups, dips and, of course, smoothies—so it is a good investment, and you don't need to spend a heap of money. If you already have a blender, try it out and see how you go making smoothies. You might need to adjust your ingredients slightly to get the right consistency. We suggest using a little more liquid and blending your greens and liquid first before adding the other ingredients. You may also need to add ingredients gradually so you don't overpower the motor of the blender, or a little more liquid to achieve the right consistency, which may be necessary no matter what type of blender you own.

While we each own a commercial-quality high-speed blender, we have been using them daily for over six years so, for us, it's been 100 per cent worth the investment. At the end of the day, the most important thing to do is just start. Remember, you can always upgrade later.

Isn't healthy eating expensive?

We generally use everyday fridge, pantry and freezer ingredients that are readily available at the supermarket, or your local fruit and veggie shop. When it comes to produce, our tip is to select recipes containing fruit and veggies that are currently in season. Not only does the price come down because there's a lot of it around, but it generally tastes better—a ripe, juicy mango with its fragrant summery smell will always win out over a mango purchased in winter and lacking that bursting-with-ripeness flavour.

Why are greens so important?

Green vegetables are high in vitamins and minerals, fibre, proteins, antioxidants, fat-burning compounds and healthy bacteria. They are also low in kilojoules (calories). The nutrients from green leafy vegetables can help protect your body from illness, cleanse your kidneys and feed your brain. They help your body maintain good health, clearer skin and shinier hair, build leaner muscles and ensure healthy digestion.

I want to lose weight. What should I do to lose a few kilos?

Losing weight is a common goal for many people. The first thing we recommend is to always consult a doctor or your healthcare practitioner before starting any type of weight-loss regimen. While we believe that eating clean, lean, balanced and nutritious meals is more important than counting calories, if you do want to watch your calories, check the kilojoule (calorie) count we provide for all our meals.

Since you want to lose weight, we recommend choosing a few meals that add up to 6275 kilojoules (1500 calories) a day, before shifting to a 5000-kilojoule (1200-calorie) meal plan when you feel ready. It's also important to get in at least half an hour of movement every day. Try going for a long walk, taking a bike ride or swimming laps. Wearing an activity tracker on your wrist is a great way to keep tabs on how much you're moving and to help you reach your fitness goals each day.

Can green smoothies help with weight loss?

Absolutely! If you want to lose weight, then green smoothies are such a good way to go about it. They can kickstart your digestion, reduce bad cholesterol, increase your energy, regulate and improve bowel movements, help you burn excess fat and decrease cravings for processed, sugary foods. Smoothies are packed with nutrients, vitamins and fibre. They're filling and tasty, making them an easy lifestyle change to make.

You're not eating processed 'diet' food; rather, you're consuming real food. Living food. Good food. Food that nourishes. Most of us have started a diet on Monday only to find ourselves binge-eating wildly like a half-starved animal by Wednesday. Because smoothies taste great and are easy to make, they offer a sustainable weight-loss method when combined with a balanced, nutritious diet and exercise.

I'm really busy and often don't have a lot of time for preparing meals. Are your recipes quick and easy to follow?

Our recipes are easy—super easy! We've created delicious meals that are simple to prepare so you won't need to be in the kitchen for hours on end.

We've also designed whole sections to help anyone who is time-poor—one-pot recipes have the added bonus of less washing up, and sheet-pan recipes let you get on with other things while the oven does the work for you.

Of all the recipes, the smoothies are the quickest to prepare, so these are a great option if you're rushed in the morning. While some of the salads and bowls require you to cook a couple of things, we try to keep it as simple as possible. That's what this book is all about. One thing we also like to do is cook in big batches and store leftovers in airtight containers in the fridge or freezer. We also like to use microwave rice and quinoa, and pre-bagged salad greens from the supermarket to speed things up.

I've heard that too much sugar is bad for you. Do your recipes include refined sugar?

Almost all the recipes in this book contain no refined sugar (such as white sugar). When a little sweetening is required, we mostly use natural sweeteners, such as honey, or sugar substitutes, such as stevia.

Should I add a green powder to my diet?

A green superfood powder is a great way to supplement your diet with added nutrients, superfoods, prebiotics and probiotics. It can help increase your energy, improve your immunity and digestion, strengthen your hair and nails, and make your skin glow.

There are plenty of brands on the market. We like our own, which we created. We use SWIISH WELLNESS SUPERGREEN Superfood Powder in smoothies, sprinkle it on yoghurt, add it to snack balls or simply stir it into a glass of water. It contains over 40 ingredients so you're benefiting from a wide variety of veggies, fruit, superfoods, pre- and probiotics. You can pick it up from shop.swiish.com.

I can't have gluten. Do your recipes contain gluten?

We've included heaps of gluten-free recipes in this book. To make things easier for you, there's a 'GF' label at the top of each recipe to indicate if it is gluten-free.

I'm following a keto diet. Are your recipes keto-friendly?

The ketogenic diet is based around the idea that you minimise carbs and instead consume a high-fat diet. The body is then forced to burn fat rather than carbs.

There are plenty of recipes in this book that contain keto-friendly ingredients such as fish, eggs, chicken, red meat, avocado, coconut, raspberries, tomatoes, cottage cheese, walnuts and almonds.

If I have a food allergy or an intolerance, can I swap out the ingredient?

Of course! Typical allergies include ingredients like nuts and seafood, while intolerances often include gluten, dairy and soy. If nuts are an issue for you, simply omit them from the recipe and perhaps try substitutes such as pumpkin seeds (pepitas), sesame seeds or chia seeds. If a recipe calls for nut butter, try using tahini instead. You may need to add some salt and a sweetener of your choice to achieve the desired taste. If a recipe contains gluten, you can always swap for gluten-free substitutes, such as buckwheat pasta, brown rice and gluten-free bread or flour.

I've heard that it's important to be 'alkaline'. What is this? And how can I become alkaline?

Basically, alkaline is the internal state in which your immune system, your cells and all the chemical reactions inside them are working with maximum efficiency. Your body is said to be at its healthiest when your insides are working in an alkaline environment, as opposed to an acidic one. The fastest way to get alkaline is to increase your daily veggie intake as much as you can. Dieticians recommend you eat 5 to 7 servings of vegetables daily. Enjoy a smoothie or smoothie bowl plus one of our superfood salads each day and your body will quickly become more alkaline.

I'm a vegetarian. Are there recipes for me?

Of course! There are plenty of vegetarian dishes to choose from. If a recipe you like calls for meat, you also have the option to drop it, or swap it for a vegetarian alternative such as eggs, tofu, lentils, chickpeas (garbanzo beans), cooked beans or tempeh. Keep in mind that cooking times will vary for these ingredients.

How do I get my kids to eat more vegetables?

Hide them! We often sneak greens into our kids' meals, and drinking a smoothie is a great way for little ones to get lots of tasty goodness in a glass. But if a smoothie recipe calls for matcha powder, green tea or coffee (these contain caffeine), or protein powder, simply omit them, as they should not be consumed by children.

There are some ingredients listed in your recipes I've never bought before. Where is the best place to look?

OK, we admit it—we use a lot of superfoods! The good news is that these days most, if not all, are available from supermarkets or health-food stores. They might cost a fraction more than your usual fruit and veggies, but we believe that it's better to invest in good health now, and live the best life you can.

Can I use frozen ingredients in my smoothies?

Yes! Most of your ingredients can be frozen—in particular, baby spinach, kale, broccoli, banana, pineapple, mango and berries. It's nice to have at least one frozen ingredient in your smoothie because cold ingredients will make it taste better.

Why do you have smoothies?

Well, having a smoothie a day was one of the easiest and simplest changes we made to our diet, and what we gained in return was a whole lot of nutrients, resulting in weight loss and more energy, clearer skin, shinier hair, better sleep, and improved digestion and immunity. We also found it removed our cravings for sugar and processed foods. There is no way we could sit down and eat that many greens in one go, so blending them into a smoothie is the perfect solution.

Why do you drink smoothies instead of juices?

Juices and smoothies are both great for your health. A juice contains only the liquid extracted from a fruit or vegetable and, although it contains very little dietary fibre, it still contains vitamins and nutrients. A smoothie, on the other hand, has the lot—fibre, vitamins and nutrients. The fibre keeps you feeling full for longer too, so it can help stop you from snacking, which also means that a smoothie is a great meal replacement.

Are smoothies a meal replacement?

Yes, definitely, they can be. We suggest you replace a meal where you tend to make poor choices or struggle to eat well. For us, during the week, that meal is breakfast, simply because we're rushing to get ready and out the door.

Everyone is different, though. We have a friend who struggled to eat well at dinner and would spend the evening wandering between the fridge and pantry, grabbing whatever she could get her hands on. For her, swapping dinner for a smoothie was a no-brainer. She's lost 8 kilograms (17½ lb), she's sleeping well and she's feeling great.

I don't have time to make a smoothie every day. Can I make a bigger batch and refrigerate or freeze it?

Yes, you can; however, smoothies only last in the fridge for about 24 hours. After that they lose some nutrients and won't taste as fresh. Instead, we suggest you divide a big batch into daily portions then freeze them in airtight containers or glass jars (just be careful to leave some space at the top of the jar as the smoothie will expand as it freezes). Thaw your smoothie in the fridge the night before you want to drink it, and by morning it'll be ready to go. To give it a fresh shot of zing and an extra flavour boost, you can add a little chlorophyll, lemon, lime or herbs.

Can you suggest a swap for bananas in smoothies?

We sometimes use bananas in our smoothies because they provide the perfect dense and creamy base; however, if you don't like bananas or prefer a low-sugar substitute, you can try using berries, pear, apple, peach, nectarines, pureed pumpkin (squash), avocado or melons—such as rockmelon (cantaloupe), honeydew or watermelon—instead. These will keep your smoothies tasty without adding the sugar spike.

What time of day is best to have a smoothie?

Whatever time you want. There is no 'best' time: you can have one for breakfast, lunch, dinner or as a snack during the day.

What do the codes at the beginning of each recipe mean?

We've added codes for each recipe, so you can see at a glance if it suits your dietary requirements. These tags are based on the ingredients list and don't include the 'toppings we've used' or elements labelled 'optional'.

* **DF** – dairy-free
* **GF** – gluten-free
* **RSF** – refined sugar-free
* **V** – vegan
* **VG** – vegetarian
* **P** – paleo

CUP AND TABLESPOON MEASURES: We have used Australian cup measures, of 250 ml (9 fl oz). Please note that the US and UK cup measures are slightly smaller, approximately 235 ml (7¾ fl oz). We have also used 20 ml (4 teaspoon) tablespoon measures. If you are using a 15 ml (3 teaspoon) tablespoon, add an extra teaspoon of the ingredient for each tablespoon specified.

OVEN GUIDE: For fan-forced ovens, as a general rule, set the oven temperature to 20°C (35°F) lower than indicated in the recipe.

Get ready

If you've been with us from the early days of *Super Green Smoothies*, you'll know we love our fruit and veggies. If you're just joining us, then you're about to discover that we *looove* fresh produce and turning it into fast, easy, delicious meals that leave you feeling satisfied and happy.

Over the years, we've developed an excellent sense of which fruit and veggies we need. We know the shortcuts, how to save money and where the investment in good-quality produce makes the difference. Either way, fruit and veggies are nutritious and, if you prepare them using our recipes, they'll always be delicious.

But we know that delicious, nutritious food sometimes falls into the too-hard basket. Everyone is busy, and the first thing we seem to neglect is nourishment. The good news is that eating well doesn't have to be complicated, expensive or time-consuming—in fact, it can be super easy.

Below, we've listed some of the items we regard as our fridge and freezer staples. Whether you're whipping up a smoothie, a bowl, a sheet-pan dinner or a one-pot meal, you'll need to have these items on hand . . .

Fridge and freezer

Avocados

Adding a bit of avo is always worth it, even if it does set you back a few extra dollars. This creamy, totally delicious fruit is full of healthy fats, which are great for your hair, skin and nails. You'll see avocado added to our smoothies, included in bowls and used as a great side dish with sheet-pan meals.

Baby greens

What started off as a baby spinach obsession has led to us using all sorts of baby leaves. It's quite common now to find baby kale, baby rocket (arugula), baby bok choy (pak choy) and lots of others at your local green grocer or supermarket. Baby greens tend to be a lot sweeter than their larger siblings, but still full of all the vitamins and minerals you need for increasing vitality, restoring energy and improving the quality of your blood. We keep baby spinach and kale in the freezer for smoothies but almost everything else we keep in the fridge.

Bananas

Sweet, delicious and totally satisfying, bananas are the ultimate energy food. They are rich in potassium, an essential mineral for maintaining healthy blood pressure and heart function. Don't keep your bananas in the fridge, though—they'll go brown! Instead, keep some in a fruit bowl and others chopped up in zip-lock bags in the freezer to use for smoothies, whips or 'nice cream'.

Berries

Berries are a fast, easy way to get a tasty hit of antioxidants and nutrients all in one mouthful. When they're not in season, stock up on frozen berries—they're just as good for you and work perfectly in smoothies. You can use fresh ones as a topping in smoothie bowls, but keep them in the fridge so they last longer.

Broccoli and broccolini

When it comes to broccoli you need to think beyond the soggy boiled broccoli your grandma may have made. Broccoli is one of the most adaptable vegetables. It goes well in smoothies, salads and curries, and can be used as a base for tabouli. Full of dietary fibre, minerals and vitamins A, B and E, it's perfect for supercharging any meal. Keep it in the fridge so it stays fresh, or chop it up and store it in zip-lock bags in the freezer—perfect for making smoothies. Broccolini is also a delicious addition to salads, one-tray meals or simply as a side dish.

Cauliflower

Cauliflower is one of those ultra-versatile veggies that can be turned into just about anything you like. We regularly use it in smoothies, and as an awesome rice substitute. It's low in kilojoules (calories) and carbs, and full of nutrients such as omega-3 fatty acids, choline, fibre, manganese, biotin and phosphorus. Always keep cauliflower in your fridge so it stays fresh.

Cheese

Which kind of cheese, you ask? Every kind, we say! We love feta, goat's cheese and haloumi. These cheeses work beautifully with salads and one-pot meals, and if we could add them to smoothies we would . . .

Coconut water

We like to keep coconut water handy to use in smoothies or just to drink on its own. It's rich in electrolytes, which makes it ultra-hydrating. Look for versions that contain no added sugar.

Eggs

Packed full of vitamins, minerals, high-quality proteins and good fats, eggs are little nutritional powerhouses. Egg is also the one ingredient that seems to turn up in breakfast, lunch, dinner and dessert, so it's a good idea to have some handy.

Fermented foods

If you have poor digestion, fermented and cultured foods can help enormously. They promote the growth of healthy bacteria in the gut, which results in better digestion and a clearer elimination system. You can find these foods in the form of pickles, kimchi, kefir, kombucha and sauerkraut. Keep them in the fridge.

Fresh herbs

Herbs are a must-have for any kitchen, perfect for adding a tonne of flavour. We use them in smoothies, but also extensively with sheet-pan and one-pot meals, salads, bowls and . . . basically everything! They add a hit of freshness and a pop of colour to roasted meals. Herbs not only finish off a dish but also make it taste special.

Ghee

Ghee is clarified butter, which means simply that it is butter with the milk solids removed. If you're sensitive to dairy products, you may find ghee to be a suitable alternative. It's also a stable oil for cooking, more so than butter—which means it can tolerate higher temperatures when cooking. While ghee adds tonnes of flavour when cooking (it's a more concentrated kind of butter flavour), just be aware that it does have a slightly higher kilojoule (calorie) count and fat content.

Kale

Kale has fast become one of the most popular greens you can buy. It is slightly more nutrient-dense than spinach but also a bit tougher. If we're using it in a salad, we like to remove the stalks, then massage the leaves with a bit of olive or coconut oil first. This helps to soften the leaves a little and also makes them easier to eat. For smoothies, just throw the leaves straight into the blender. Keep your kale in the fridge, but if you have purchased the bagged variety chopped into ribbons and find you haven't used it all, keep it in the freezer and use it in your smoothies.

Medjool dates

Medjool dates are our choice because they're super sweet and soft. They're also very high in fibre, which helps you feel full for longer. We use dates in brekkie bowls, smoothies and snacks.

Non-dairy milk

Plant-based milk isn't just for vegans and those who are lactose-intolerant. Soy milk is high in protein, and unsweetened almond milk is low in kilojoules (calories). These are both great alternatives to use in smoothies and cooked dishes. Hazelnut milk is full of vitamin B, and coconut milk is rich in vitamins, minerals and fibre; both are great as a substitute for thin (pouring) cream due to their similar consistency. When it comes to coconut milk, with the recipes in this book, be sure to check whether we refer to the carton variety (lower in calories and typically mixed with water or other nut milks) or the tinned variety (higher in calories and fat as it's extracted from the coconut meat without being diluted). Also be sure to read the labels so you choose milks without added sugars and flavours.

Pomegranate seeds

A few years ago, pomegranates weren't a hugely popular fruit. Now the seeds find their way into all sorts of dishes. Known for their antioxidant, antiviral and anti-tumour properties, pomegranate seeds are amazing for your health. We love to keep them on hand so we can throw them into smoothies or to add them to salads or brekkie bowls.

Red cabbage

We're always looking for ways to introduce more colour into our diet, which is why red cabbage has become a staple for us. Mix it with leafy greens to form a salad base, and add it to stir-fries. Another great thing about cabbage is that, when it's too old to be eaten fresh, you can chop it up and ferment it in a jar. It will then keep for weeks in the fridge.

Tahini

Not used as much as it should be, tahini is an oily paste made from finely ground sesame seeds. Full of vitamins, it is a richer source of protein than milk, sunflower seeds, soy beans and most nuts. Use it to make your own hummus, drizzle it on a salad, or even spread it on toast.

Turmeric

Turmeric is one of our favourite spices, not only for the flavour it adds to cooking, but also for its many health benefits. Known for its anti-inflammatory properties, turmeric also aids in increasing immunity and protecting against illness. Turmeric's phytochemicals boost the function of cells, organs and tissues. You can use turmeric in curries, scrambled eggs, sprinkled over veggies for roasting, in soups, smoothies or lattés (yep, turmeric lattés are a thing—and they're delicious!).

Yoghurt

One thing we always have on hand is a tub of good-quality yoghurt, so we can add it to smoothies, or use it with overnight oats or for dressings. Yoghurt is full of live, active cultures that help to balance the microflora in your intestines and keep your tummy happy. We like Greek-style yoghurt and coconut yoghurt.

Pantry

If you want to live a healthy lifestyle, prepping your pantry is key. Keeping your cupboards full of clean, nutrition-rich ingredients will not only prevent you from eating unhealthy snacks but also help keep you motivated to maintain a healthy diet.

Over the years, the list of items we consider pantry essentials has definitely expanded. With new knowledge about what's nutritious and what's not constantly emerging, people are beginning to question whether some staples still belong in their pantry. What were once considered rare and hard-to-find superfoods have now been given their own section in the supermarket. Many sugars are being replaced with natural sweeteners and fat (good fat) is once again our friend. As a result, most pantries need an update.

While we use hundreds of different ingredients in this book, you'll find there are some that pop up over and over again. To make things easier for you, we've put together a list of our pantry staples.

Acai

Said to be one of the most nutritious berries on earth, acai is high in the antioxidant anthocyanin, which may help to protect against high levels of cholesterol in the bloodstream and free radical damage. It's also known as an immunity booster, digestive aid and an energy booster; plus it's super delicious. You can pick up acai in powdered form to add to cereal or yoghurt, or frozen ready to blend into smoothies. Yum!

Almond meal

Almond meal is a fantastic, low-carb alternative to wheat flour because it's high in protein and good fats but free of gluten. You can buy it from the supermarket, or make your own by processing almonds to crumbs and storing them in an airtight container in the fridge.

Apple cider vinegar

This tangy liquid is a definite pantry must-have. Not only is it a great addition to marinades, dressings and sauces, it's amazing for your health too. Apple cider vinegar can help to regulate blood sugar, delay the effects of ageing and promote weight loss. It's important to check with your doctor if you have diabetes or insulin sensitivity but, for otherwise healthy people, we recommend drinking a teaspoon or two mixed with a glass of water every morning.

Black rice

Black rice has been eaten in regions of Asia for thousands of years. Today this type of rice is gaining popularity as people discover all its amazing health benefits. You can find it in sushi trains, restaurants and health-food stores all over Australia. Some supermarkets even stock it in the ultra-convenient microwave variety. Of all the rice types, black rice is the richest in powerful disease-fighting antioxidants. It's also loaded with fibre and may help stop the development of diabetes, cancer and heart disease; it can even prevent weight gain. We love it in poke bowls and as a nutritious side dish.

Brown rice

We substitute brown rice for white rice when we can. It has a lovely nutty and chewy texture that seems to go well with everything. It's also high in complex carbohydrates and full of hunger-busting fibre.

Buckwheat noodles

Buckwheat or soba noodles are a great alternative to regular noodles as they have a low glycaemic index (meaning the body uses the energy more slowly) and are usually gluten-free. They're also super easy to cook. You just pop them in a bowl of hot water for a few minutes, drain them and they're done. You can then toss them through salads, add them to stir-fries or eat them as you would regular noodles.

Cacao powder

Most people who like to bake have a box of cocoa powder in their pantry, but if you want to up the nutritional value, then try cacao powder instead. It's perfect for adding that yummy, chocolatey taste to smoothies, snacks and desserts.

Chia seeds

Rich in antioxidants, chia seeds are an excellent source of omega-3 fatty acids and provide fibre, iron and calcium, so they had to make it onto our essentials list. You can use them in many different breakfast, smoothie, dessert and snack recipes, or sprinkle them over salads.

Coconut oil

Coconut oil is our favourite alternative to olive oil, and for good reason. It's rich in essential fatty acids, it's great for your hair and skin, and it can be used in just about any recipe. It also tastes delicious.

Collagen powder

Collagen is the most abundant protein in the body—it's found in your skin, muscles, blood, bones, cartilage and ligaments. However, collagen production declines as you get older, just when you need it most for glowing skin and strong, healthy bones and joints. Adding collagen to your daily diet is a no-brainer. It promotes skin elasticity, helps reduces wrinkles and combat skin dryness. We use our SWIISH WELLNESS GLOW Marine Collagen Powder in smoothies, glow bowls and overnight oats for that added boost of skin-loving goodness.

Herbs and spices

Put simply, herbs and spices are the key to adding maximum flavour to any dish. Most of them are quite high in antioxidants, and the hotter kinds of spice, in particular, can help speed up your metabolism. Cinnamon and nutmeg are our favourites when it comes to making sweeter dishes, while turmeric, coriander, cumin, rosemary and basil are great for salads, curries and soups.

Maca powder

A deliciously nutty flavour is what you can expect from maca powder, which is made from the root of the maca plant. Add it to smoothies and desserts for a slightly sweet, nutty flavour.

Matcha powder

Made up of ground green tea leaves, matcha is filled with antioxidants. Mix it with yoghurt, add it to smoothies or add it to protein balls and bars for an extra metabolism boost.

Nuts

Nuts are full of good fats that help you feel full, making them the perfect snack to keep in your pantry. Almonds are our favourite because they're one of the lower kilojoule (calorie) options, and they taste delicious when roasted and sprinkled with a bit of pink salt.

Nut butters

Most people will have a jar of peanut butter in their pantry; we prefer to use all-natural almond, cashew or hazelnut butter instead. Not only are nut butters packed full of good fats and protein but you can use them in just about everything—smoothies, sauces, baking, bliss balls—or spread on toast. Our favourite way to eat nut butter is to smear it all over a banana or apple slices. Trust us, it's amazing.

Oats

Rolled (porridge) oats can be used in many different ways. Cook them for breakfast, add them to smoothies to keep you feeling full for longer, use them to make biscuits (cookies), or grind them into flour. They're rich in complex carbohydrates and taste absolutely delicious.

Pomegranate molasses

You'll find pomegranate molasses (which is essentially pomegranate juice that has been reduced down to a syrup) at the supermarket or specialty grocers. You don't need to use much, and you'll find it adds a tangy depth of flavour to salad dressings or even drizzled over roasted veggies. You can also add it to iced teas or sparkling water for a refreshing treat.

Quinoa

This grain-like seed is a must-have for any pantry. It's the perfect high-protein, gluten-free alternative to the usual pasta and rice. Believe it or not, you can even use it to make porridge. It tastes delicious.

Rice malt syrup

This syrup pops up in a lot of our recipes. That's because it's probably the most nutritious sugar swap available. Made from 100 per cent organic brown rice, this sweet syrup is high in complex carbohydrates and is completely fructose-free. It's fantastic for making snacks, or adding to salad dressings in place of sugar.

Stevia

If you're trying to cut down on sugar in your diet, you have to keep some of this plant-based sweetener in the house (or in your handbag for coffee on the go). Stevia is an all-natural, zero-kilojoule (calorie) substitute for sugar.

Superfood powder

These days, having a green superfood powder in your pantry is the norm. There are lots of brands on the market but we like to use the one we created. We add SWIISH WELLNESS SUPERGREEN Superfood Powder to smoothies, sprinkle it on yoghurt, add it to snack balls and mix it in with a bottle of water to drink on the go. Keeping superfood powder in plain sight in your pantry will mean you're more likely to use it.

Vanilla

As we learn more about the importance of sticking to natural foods, vanilla bean paste and vanilla extract are taking the place of vanilla essence. While many types of vanilla essence are chemically manufactured flavourings, vanilla bean paste and vanilla extract are natural products derived from vanilla beans. We love using the sweet paste or syrupy extract in smoothies, breakfast dishes, healthy snacks and desserts. You would typically use vanilla bean paste where a recipe calls for a vanilla pod with the seeds scraped out (it's so much easier!). However vanilla extract and vanilla bean paste are basically the same from a flavour and intensity point of view, so keep an eye out for whichever is on special at the supermarket.

Za'atar

This delicious savoury spice is a blend of ingredients, typically including sesame seeds, sumac, thyme and salt. Aside from being ultra-delicious as a sprinkle over roast veggies and salads, as a marinade for chicken, meat or fish, it is also delicious simply eaten with pita bread dipped in olive oil as a snack. The ingredients have powerful properties, including being great for increasing immunity, fighting inflammation and providing the body with antioxidants.

Super-easy tips

When it comes to staying lean, healthy and strong, it doesn't have to be hard or time-consuming. You just need to be organised and use shortcuts. And who doesn't love a good shortcut? Our tips for cutting corners will save you time and money and, quite often, washing up! They will also help you get on—and then stay on—the healthy path, fuss-free.

Be prepared

Before you start preparing food, always make sure you have the right equipment. The basic tools you need are a blender, food processor, sharp knife, grater and peeler. Food processors are quite inexpensive these days and can take a lot of the hassle out of chopping vegetables.

When it comes to your blender it's good to know its strength, as this will determine how much you need to pre-chop your ingredients. The more powerful your blender, the less you need to chop before blending. If you don't have a high-powered commercial-grade blender, you might have a hard time creating a smooth consistency (which some recipes may call for). In this case, simply chop tougher ingredients like broccoli into smaller pieces to make it easier for your blender to break them down.

Take shortcuts

Washing, chopping, grating and slicing can take up a lot of time. It's perfectly OK to buy pre-washed and bagged baby spinach, kale, other leafy greens and rainbow salads. Pick up bags of pre-cut carrot and celery sticks and stir-fry veggies, which are available at most supermarkets. Use 90-second microwave rice or quinoa or couscous to save time. We also use tinned beans, rather than preparing them from scratch. We simply rinse them first before using them. When boiling eggs, we cook a few at once and store them in the fridge for a couple of days.

Pre-portion

When it comes to dishes you'll be making fresh on a daily basis, it helps to pre-portion ingredients. For example, if you make a smoothie every day, try dividing leafy greens into 1- or 2-cup portions to take the time out of measuring. Berries, broccoli and cauliflower can be separated into ½-cup portions, while larger fruits, avocado, lemons and limes are best stored in quarters.

Goodness all year round

Just because your favourite fruits or vegetables aren't in season doesn't mean you have to miss out. Frozen and tinned are totally acceptable options. We like to buy frozen mango and berries from the supermarket to enjoy all year round. Frozen fruits and vegetables taste just as great and last longer, plus they still contain all the nutrients you need. Tinned pineapple is OK when no fresh ripe pineapple is available. Just make sure it's in natural juice with no added sugar, and drain off its juice before freezing.

Adaptogens

Adapt-o-what? Before you wonder if you somehow ended up opening a chemistry textbook instead of a cookbook, hear us out.

There's a lot of buzz around adaptogens right now—and for good reason. It's no secret that so many people get through each day with the help of plenty of caffeine and sugar. From the early morning double-shot latté to the mid-morning muffins to the afternoon chocolate hit, the one thing we hear time and time again is that everyone is tired and stressed out, and that they use coffee and sugar to give them a lift.

As we've already said, our lives are busier than they've ever been. Every single day there are so many demands placed on our bodies that it's no wonder some of us struggle to cope, then turn to what we perceive to be quick fixes.

The thing is: it's a never-ending cycle and it doesn't really work. The sugar crash is real, and too much caffeine can disrupt your sleeping patterns and stop you from getting quality sleep.

The solution lies in your diet, and specifically in adaptogens. These are basically herbs, plants and roots that restore balance in your body. Over time— read: they aren't a quick fix—they can help your body to deal with stress and fight fatigue in a way that's gentle, without the highs and lows you get from sugar or caffeine. And managing stress in the body allows cells to better use oxygen while also providing you with more energy.

Many adaptogenic herbs, such as holy basil, have been used for centuries in traditional Chinese and Ayurvedic medicines. And while more research into adaptogens is being conducted, it's worth considering including them in your diet. Just bear in mind that everyone reacts differently to adaptogenic foods, so always have a chat to your healthcare professional before using them, especially if you're pregnant or breastfeeding.

Looking for somewhere to start? Try reishi mushroom, shiitake mushroom, licorice root, ashwagandha (Indian ginseng), holy basil, sea buckthorn and maca. You can find these at health-food shops where you'll find many of them sold as teas, supplements or powders.

You can also make our maca date smoothie, over the page.

MACA DATE SMOOTHIE

DF // GF // RSF // V // VG // P // 1643 KJ/393 CAL PER SERVE
SERVES 1

375 ml (13 fl oz/1½ cups)
unsweetened almond milk
½ frozen banana, chopped
3 medjool dates, pitted
2 teaspoons nut butter
60 g (2¼ oz/½ cup) cauliflower
florets
1 teaspoon vanilla extract or
vanilla bean paste
1 tablespoon maca powder

Put all the ingredients in a blender and process until smooth. Before serving, we garnished ours with an extra swirl of nut butter and a slice of banana.

Sheet-pan (one-tray) tricks

If you're thinking, 'Oh sheet, what's the fuss about sheet-pan dinners?', let us explain. A sheet-pan dinner is where everything is roasted together on one baking tray. It's an absolute weeknight go-to for us, and not just because it means fewer dishes to wash. A sheet-pan dinner that's done right is just as delicious as any meal you might have spent hours, and way more pots and pans, creating.

But if you think all you'll need to do is turn your oven on and throw some stuff on a baking tray, you're wrong. There are a few tips and tricks we have in our apron pocket to share with you.

1 Buy a flat baking tray that fits

This might sound obvious, but ovens are all different sizes and so are baking trays. Buy the biggest one that will fit in your oven so you can fit more on it.

2 Let your tray heat up along with your oven

To speed up the cooking time, and ensure that your dinner gets going immediately, stick your baking tray in the oven as it preheats. By the time you're ready to add the food, the tray will be sizzling-hot. Just remember to be careful when handling it.

3 Line up, line up

Line the tray with foil or baking paper to help make cleaning up easy. Remember: if you're grilling (broiling) at the end, do not use baking paper, as it can catch alight. Go with foil, and give it a spray with an olive or coconut oil cooking spray to prevent food from sticking to it.

4 Be a matchmaker

To build the best sheet-pan dinner you need to get smart with matchmaking ingredients. You want to use protein (like chicken, fish, red meat) that needs the same cooking time as the veggies you've paired it with. Otherwise you'll end up with perfectly cooked chicken but burnt veggies, or vice versa.

5 Sometimes two trays are better than one

Don't torture yourself trying to fit everything onto one baking tray just so you can say, 'Hey guys, look at me . . . I cooked this whole thing on one tray' (insert laughing emoji). Sometimes, having two trays will give you more space and more control over your cooking.

6 Take a uniform approach

Cut the vegetables into roughly the same size to ensure they cook as evenly as possible.

7 A cut above the rest

Avoid cuts of meat that need braising such as pork shoulder, beef short ribs or lamb shanks. Instead, what works better are bone-in, skin-on chicken drumsticks or thighs, pork tenderloins or cuts of beef like sirloin. Also, whole fish or fish fillets work well, as does a rack of lamb or lamb chops. For vegetarians, tofu is delicious roasted in the oven. Beans are perfect for sheet-pan dinners, and eggs are also a winner.

8 Get saucy

Once you've mastered the basics, you can kick it up a notch and roast ingredients that you can turn into a sauce. For example, you can whisk cloves from a head of roasted garlic into store-bought mayo for a cheat's version of aioli, or roast and puree tomatoes for an incredible roast tomato sauce.

9 Give it a good grilling

If you want a bit of crispy skin on your chicken legs or a bit of extra crunch on your chickpeas, just turn the grill on at the end of roasting until you achieve the desired level of crispiness. The only catch here is that you can't wander off and read a good book or settle in for a season of your favourite Netflix show. You'll have to loiter and watch it carefully because it can go very quickly from perfect to burnt.

10 The finishing touches

Technically speaking, not everything has to be cooked on the baking tray for it to be a winner of a dinner. In fact, sometimes after the main part of the dish comes out of the oven we add extra elements. You'll see that we add fresh herbs, or sprinkle seeds or chopped chilli on top. These small tweaks at the end help bring the dish together and add some colour, crunch and extra flavour.

CHAPTER 1
Salads

SUMMER SUPERFOOD SALAD

GF // RSF // VG // 1898 KJ/454 CAL PER SERVE

SERVES 2

90 g (3¼ oz/2 cups) chopped
   rocket (arugula) leaves
45 g (1½ oz/1 cup) baby spinach
   leaves
25 g (1 oz/½ cup) mint leaves
30 g (1⅛ oz/¼ cup) roughly
   chopped pecans
2 tablespoons flaked almonds,
   toasted
125 g (4½ oz/1 cup) raspberries
1 small mango, diced
1 fig, sliced
100 g (3½ oz) goat's cheese,
   crumbled

DRESSING (OPTIONAL)
4 tablespoons extra virgin
   olive oil
2 tablespoons white wine
   vinegar
1 tablespoon maple syrup
pink salt and freshly ground
   black pepper

Place the salad ingredients in a serving dish.

If having the dressing, whisk together the dressing
ingredients in a small bowl.

Dress the salad and serve immediately.

TANDOORI CHICKEN WITH CUCUMBER YOGHURT SALAD

RSF // 2142 KJ/512 CAL PER SERVE
SERVES 4

8 small boneless, skinless chicken thighs, fat trimmed

2 tablespoons tandoori paste

1 tablespoon extra virgin olive oil

1 large Lebanese (short) cucumber, shredded or grated

200 g (7 oz) sweet red cherry tomatoes, sliced

390 g (13¾ oz/1½ cups) Greek-style yoghurt

50 g (1¾ oz/⅓ cup) thinly sliced red (Spanish) onion

1 jalapeno chilli, finely chopped (use half if less heat is preferred)

1 large garlic clove, crushed

2 tablespoons finely chopped flat-leaf (Italian) parsley leaves

2 tablespoons mint leaves

2 tablespoons lemon juice, plus lemon wedges to serve (optional)

Place the chicken and tandoori paste in a bowl and mix well, making sure the thighs are well coated.

Heat the olive oil in a frying pan over medium–high heat and add the chicken thighs. Cook, turning once, for 8–10 minutes until cooked through. Rest 5 minutes and slice.

While the chicken cooks, make the salad by gently mixing the remaining ingredients together on a platter. Top with the sliced chicken and serve with lemon wedges for extra flavour.

serving suggestion

★ Supermarket naan bread can be a great addition to this meal.

BLACK RICE AND MANGO SALAD

DF // RSF // V // VG // 1234 KJ/295 CAL PER SERVE

SERVES 4

1 x 250 g (9 oz) packet
90-second microwave
black rice
1 bunch of broccolini, ends
trimmed
1 red capsicum (pepper),
thinly sliced
2 spring onions (scallions),
thinly sliced
50 g (1¾ oz/2 cups) kale ribbons
(stalks removed, leaves
sliced and massaged)
1 large mango (or 2 medium
ones), sliced into wedges
lime wedges, to serve

DRESSING

125 ml (4 fl oz/½ cup) coconut
milk (tinned variety)
1 tablespoon lime juice (about
½ lime)
2 teaspoons soy sauce
1 teaspoon grated fresh ginger
1 large garlic clove, crushed
1 long red chilli, deseeded and
thinly sliced
2 teaspoons maple syrup
3 tablespoons finely chopped
coriander (cilantro) leaves

Microwave the black rice according to the packet instructions. Once cooked, place in a serving dish and set aside to cool.

Next, place all the dressing ingredients in a small jug or jar, stir and set aside to allow all the flavours to combine.

Blanch the broccolini (pop it into a heatproof bowl, cover with boiling water and set aside for 3–4 minutes, or until just cooked through). Drain and set aside to cool.

Add the capsicum, spring onion, kale and mango to the black rice. Finally, slice the broccolini lengthways and add that too. Serve with the dressing on the side and add as desired. Mix well and serve with lime wedges. Yum!

★ If you can't find the microwave version black rice just get the normal version and cook it as per packet instructions—still very easy!

CHICKEN SHAWARMA SALAD

DF // GF // RSF // P // 1996 KJ/478 CAL PER SERVE
SERVES 4

2 tablespoons Middle Eastern
   spice mix
2 tablespoons extra virgin
   olive oil
1 lemon, zested and juiced
500 g (1 lb 2 oz) boneless,
   skinless chicken thighs,
   fat trimmed
1 butter lettuce, leaves roughly
   chopped
25 g (1 oz/½ cup) small mint
   leaves
250 g (9 oz) cherry tomato
   medley, sliced
1 Lebanese (short) cucumber,
   sliced
½ small red (Spanish) onion,
   thinly sliced

DRESSING

135 g (4¾ oz/½ cup) tahini
3 tablespoons extra virgin
   olive oil
2 lemons, zested and juiced
3 tablespoons hot water,
   plus 3 tablespoons extra
   if needed
pink salt and freshly ground
   black pepper

Combine the spice mix, olive oil and lemon zest and juice in a shallow container. Add the chicken and mix well. Cover and marinate in the fridge for 20–30 minutes (or overnight if you wish).

Chargrill or pan-fry the chicken over medium heat until cooked through, 6–8 minutes on each side.

While the chicken is cooking, make the dressing. Combine the tahini, olive oil and lemon zest and juice in a small bowl and whisk in 3 tablespoons of hot water. If you like your dressing a bit runnier, whisk in the extra water. Season with salt and pepper.

Rest the chicken for 5 minutes and slice.

Scatter the lettuce and mint on a platter. Layer the tomato slices, cucumber and onion over the salad base. Top with the chicken, then drizzle over the tahini dressing. Serve immediately.

THREE CHEERS MEXICAN CORN SALAD

GF // RSF // VG // 1892 KJ/453 CAL PER SERVE
SERVES 3

3 corn cobs
1 teaspoon extra virgin olive oil
150 g (5½ oz) Danish feta
1 small green chilli, deseeded
    and thinly sliced
25 g (1 oz/½ cup) finely
    chopped coriander (cilantro)
    leaves
2 spring onions (scallions),
    thinly sliced
½ red (Spanish) onion, finely
    diced
1 avocado, diced
1 lime, halved, to serve

DRESSING (OPTIONAL)
3 tablespoons light sour cream
3 tablespoons lime juice
½ teaspoon smoked paprika
¼ teaspoon cayenne pepper
    (add another ¼ teaspoon
    if you like it extra hot)
¼ teaspoon pink salt

To start on the salad, use a sharp knife to carefully slice the kernels off the corn cobs into a bowl. Heat the olive oil in a frying pan over medium–high heat. Add the corn and cook, stirring often (this helps it to get a good char), until golden brown, about 3–4 minutes. Set aside to cool slightly.

Meanwhile, add the remaining salad ingredients to a serving bowl.

Combine all the dressing ingredients in a small bowl and use a fork or whisk to mix well.

Add the corn to the salad and toss well. Squeeze a little lime juice over the salad. Serve with the dressing and the remaining lime on the side.

We called this our Three Cheers Mexican Corn Salad because every time we make it, it gets devoured and then we all say 'Three cheers to the cook!', hence the name. — Maha

FAST AND EASY SNAPPER
WITH PEACH SALSA

DF // GF // RSF // P // 1505 KJ/360 CAL PER SERVE
SERVES 2

2 yellow peaches, unpeeled, diced
1 Lebanese (short) cucumber, diced
2 spring onions (scallions), thinly sliced
1 long green chilli, deseeded and diced
25 g (1 oz/½ cup) finely chopped coriander (cilantro) leaves, plus extra sprigs to serve (optional)
1 lime, juiced
pink salt and freshly ground black pepper
2 x 200 g (7¼ oz) snapper fillets, skin on
1 tablespoon extra virgin olive oil

Make the salsa by combining the peach, cucumber, spring onion, chilli and coriander in a bowl. Add half the lime juice, season with salt and pepper and taste. We love ours extra zingy, so if you do too, add the remaining lime juice.

Season the snapper with salt and pepper. Heat the olive oil in a frying pan over medium–high heat and cook the fish, skin side down, for 3–4 minutes. Turn and continue cooking for another minute or two, until the middle of the fish is opaque.

Plate the fish and serve with the salsa on the side, garnished with extra sprigs of coriander as desired.

EUROPEAN SUMMER NIGHTS SALAD

RSF // VG // 2219 KJ/531 CAL PER SERVE

SERVES 4

225 g (8 oz/1½ cups) risoni

3 tablespoons extra virgin
olive oil

2 spring onions (scallions),
thinly sliced

30 g (1 oz/1 cup) roughly
chopped flat-leaf (Italian)
parsley leaves

40 g (1½ oz/⅓ cup) roughly
chopped walnuts

3 tablespoons pitted and
quartered kalamata olives

60 g (2¼ oz/⅓ cup) dried raisins
or dried cranberries

100 g (3½ oz) feta, crumbled

1 lemon, zested, plus juice and
wedges to serve (optional)

pink salt and freshly ground
black pepper

Cook the risoni according to the packet instructions. Drain well. Drizzle over 1 tablespoon of olive oil and stir through (this helps it to not stick together). Set aside.

Next, place the spring onion, parsley, walnuts, olives, raisins or cranberries, feta and lemon zest in a large serving bowl and mix everything together well. Add the risoni and stir through. Drizzle on the remaining olive oil and add a squeeze of lemon juice, if desired. Taste and season if required.

✴ This salad works beautifully with smoked trout or barbecued chicken breast. Just shred and toss into the salad. Delicious!

MIDDLE EASTERN LAMB CUTLETS WITH PEARL COUSCOUS TABOULI

DF // RSF // 2492 KJ/596 CAL PER SERVE

SERVES 4

12 lamb cutlets, French trimmed
1 tablespoon extra virgin
    olive oil

MARINADE
2 teaspoons Middle Eastern
    spice mix
2 teaspoons sumac
2 teaspoons chilli powder
2 teaspoons rice malt syrup
1½ tablespoons lemon juice
1 tablespoon tomato paste

COUSCOUS TABOULI
250 g (9 oz) pearl (big)
    couscous
pink salt and freshly ground
    black pepper
200 g (7 oz) sweet red cherry
    tomatoes, halved
2 Lebanese (short) cucumbers,
    sliced into half moons
12 prunes, pitted and sliced
3–4 spring onions (scallions),
    thinly sliced
30 g (1 oz/1 cup) finely chopped
    flat-leaf (Italian) parsley
    leaves
25 g (1 oz/½ cup) finely
    chopped mint leaves
2 tablespoons extra virgin
    olive oil
2 tablespoons lemon juice

Mix together the marinade ingredients in a bowl. Add the lamb cutlets and turn to coat thoroughly. Set aside while you crack on with the couscous tabouli.

Put the pearl couscous in a saucepan and cover with 625 ml (21½ fl oz/2½ cups) of water. Season generously with salt and pepper and place over medium–low heat. Cover with a lid and simmer, stirring occasionally, for 8–10 minutes until tender.

While that cooks, combine the tomato halves, cucumber, prunes, spring onion and herbs in a bowl.

Drain the couscous and add to the salad, along with the olive oil and lemon juice. Toss to combine and season to taste.

Heat the olive oil in a large frying pan over medium–high heat and cook the cutlets in batches for 2–3 minutes on each side for medium–rare, or for longer until cooked to your liking.

Divide the salad between serving bowls and top with the cutlets. Serve immediately.

 tip

★ If you find your couscous clumps together when you drain it, just give it a little rinse and set aside for a few minutes to drain. You can also mix in a teaspoon of extra virgin olive oil if need be.

MUMBAI NIGHTS ROAST VEGGIE SALAD

DF // GF // RSF // V // VG // 1300 KJ/311 CAL PER SERVE
SERVES 4

90 g (3¼ oz/3 cups) kale
ribbons (stalks removed,
leaves sliced and massaged)
1 x 400 g (14 oz) tin lentils,
drained and rinsed
2 tablespoons pumpkin seeds
(pepitas)
2 tablespoons golden raisins

ROAST VEGETABLES
2 small carrots, peeled and
sliced into rounds about
5 mm (¼ inch) thick
1 sweet potato, peeled and
thinly sliced into half moons
120 g (4¼ oz/2 cups) broccoli
florets
1 red capsicum (pepper),
chopped into large bite-sized
pieces
2 large red (Spanish) onions,
quartered
1 zucchini (courgette), sliced
into rounds about 1 cm
(½ inch) thick
1½ tablespoons extra virgin
olive oil
2 teaspoons curry powder
¼ teaspoon ground turmeric
good pinch of pink salt

DRESSING (OPTIONAL)
1 teaspoon rice malt syrup
3 tablespoons tahini
½ lemon, juiced
1 teaspoon extra virgin olive oil
1 garlic clove, crushed

Preheat the oven to 200°C (400°F). Line a baking tray
(or two) with baking paper.

Place all the roast vegetables ingredients in a large
bowl and toss to combine. Ensure that the veggies are
well coated with the oil, spices and salt, and add to
the baking tray. Roast for 20–25 minutes until all the
veggies can be pierced easily with a fork.

If making the dressing, combine the dressing
ingredients with 3 tablespoons of water in a small
jug or jar and stir well.

Massage the kale leaves and tip into a serving bowl.
Add the lentils and roasted veggies, gently mix
together and then top with the pumpkin seeds and
raisins. Serve immediately with the dressing (if using)
on the side.

★ This delicious dressing goes a long way, so it's best
to let everyone add as little or as much as they like.

SUPERPOWERED FOUR C SALAD

GF // RSF // VG // 1722 KJ/412 CAL PER SERVE

SERVES 2

150 g (5½ oz/2 cups) red
cabbage, finely shredded
2 carrots, shredded
250 g (9 oz/2 cups) cauliflower
florets, diced
½ red (Spanish) onion, finely
sliced
1 red apple, thinly sliced
72 g (2¾ oz/½ cup) dried
cranberries
110 g (3½ oz) goat's feta,
crumbled

DRESSING (OPTIONAL)
3 tablespoons maple syrup
½ lemon, juiced
4 tablespoons extra virgin
olive oil
pink salt and freshly ground
black pepper

Combine the cabbage, carrot, cauliflower, onion, apple and cranberries in a bowl.

If you plan to include the dressing, combine all the dressing ingredients in a bowl.

Pour the dressing over the salad and toss. Top with the crumbled goat's feta and serve.

★ Use a food processor with the slice blade to shred the cabbage and carrot. Next, dice the cauliflower in the food processor.

SPEEDY, SPICY, SMOKY SALMON AND SLAW

DF // RSF // 2074 KJ/496 CAL PER SERVE
SERVES 2

1 x 185 g (6½ oz) hot-smoked salmon fillet (available at supermarkets)
1 tablespoon toasted sesame seeds, to serve (optional)

DRESSING
4 tablespoons rice vinegar
2 tablespoons sesame oil
2 tablespoons soy sauce
2 tablespoons honey

SLAW
150 g (5½ oz/2 cups) red cabbage
150 g (5½ oz/2 cups) green cabbage
1 spring onion (scallion), trimmed
15 g (½ oz/½ cup) coriander (cilantro) leaves
10 g (¼ oz/½ cup) mint leaves
1 carrot, grated

Combine all the dressing ingredients in a bowl and set aside.

Process the slaw ingredients in a food processor or thinly slice. Place in a serving bowl.

Flake the salmon into chunks and scatter over the salad. Drizzle on a generous serve of dressing and sprinkle with sesame seeds (if using).

I've made extra dressing here as I love to have my salad very saucy. Use as little or as much as you like. — Sally

JAMAICAN JERK CHICKEN AND HERB SLAW

DF // RSF // P // 2339 KJ/560 CAL PER SERVE

SERVES 2

4 chicken drumsticks

4 tablespoons jerk seasoning

1 tablespoon extra virgin
olive oil

SLAW

150 g (5½ oz/2 cups) red
cabbage

150 g (5½ oz/2 cups) green
cabbage

1 spring onion (scallion),
trimmed

15 g (½ oz/½ cup) coriander
(cilantro) leaves

10 g (¼ oz/½ cup) mint leaves

1 carrot, grated

DRESSING (OPTIONAL)

1 teaspoon finely grated ginger

2 limes, juiced, plus extra
wedges to serve

2 tablespoons extra virgin
olive oil

1 tablespoon honey or rice
malt syrup

1 teaspoon pink salt

Preheat the oven to 200°C (400°F). Place a large sheet of baking paper on a baking tray.

Cut slits into the flesh on the drumsticks. Rub the seasoning and oil over the drumsticks, ensuring you get the seasoning into the slits. Transfer the drumsticks to the middle of the paper, bring in the sides and twist to seal the parcel. Bake for 20–25 minutes until the chicken is almost cooked through. Open up the parcel and return the chicken to the oven for 5–10 minutes to cook through and let the skin get crispy.

Process the slaw ingredients in a food processor or thinly slice. Place in a serving bowl.

Combine the dressing ingredients in a jar, shake well and drizzle over the slaw. Serve the chicken with the slaw and extra lime wedges.

PRAWN, WATERMELON AND FETA SALAD

GF // RSF // 1042 KJ/249 CAL PER SERVE

SERVES 4

½ small seedless watermelon
    (about 2.5 kg/5 lb 10 oz), skin
    removed and flesh cut into
    bite-sized pieces
20 cooked tiger prawns (shrimp)
    (about 500 g/17½ oz),
    peeled and deveined with
    tails left on
100 g (3½ oz) feta, crumbled
25 g (1 oz/½ cup) mint leaves
25 g (1 oz/½ cup) coriander
    (cilantro) leaves
1 long red chilli, deseeded and
    finely chopped
½ small red (Spanish) onion,
    thinly sliced
60 g (2¼ oz/2 packed cups)
    watercress sprigs (or salad
    leaves of your choice)
2 limes, juiced
pink salt and freshly ground
    black pepper
drizzle of extra virgin olive oil
    (optional)

Place all the ingredients on a serving platter and toss well to combine. Taste and season with more salt and pepper if needed. Add a drizzle of extra virgin olive oil if desired. Serve immediately.

CHAPTER 2

One-pot meals

MEAT-FREE MONDAY FAST FRITTATA

GF // RSF // VG // 1132 KJ/271 CAL PER SERVE
SERVES 4

2 tablespoons ghee or extra
   virgin olive oil
90 g (3¼ oz/1 cup) sliced
   mushrooms
1 leek, white and pale green part
   only, thinly sliced
2 spring onions (scallions), thinly
   sliced
pink salt and freshly ground
   black pepper
120 g (4¼ oz/4 cups) kale
   ribbons (stalks removed,
   leaves sliced and massaged)
6 eggs
125 ml (4 fl oz/½ cup) milk
65 g (2½ oz/½ cup) Danish feta,
   crumbled
basil leaves, to serve (optional)

Heat the ghee or oil in a large frying pan over medium–high heat. Add the mushrooms and cook for 3 minutes until golden brown. Remove from the pan and set aside.

Add the leek and spring onion to the pan, season with salt and pepper and pan-fry until softened, about 3 minutes. Stir in the kale and cook for 1–2 minutes until wilted.

While the kale cooks, whisk the eggs and milk together in a bowl.

Pour the egg mixture into the pan. Scatter on the mushrooms and feta and cook for 5 minutes until the edge of the frittata has set.

Preheat the grill.

Place the pan under the grill and cook for 5 minutes until the frittata has set in the middle and the feta has softened on top. Sprinkle with basil leaves before serving (as desired).

EASY ITALIAN EGGS

DF // RSF // 851 KJ/204 CAL PER SERVE
SERVES 2

---

1 tablespoon extra virgin
   olive oil
1 red (Spanish) onion, finely
   diced
3–4 garlic cloves, crushed
1½ tablespoons thyme leaves
1 x 400 g (14 oz) tin whole
   peeled tomatoes, roughly
   chopped while still in the tin
1 x 400 g (14 oz) tin cannellini
   beans, drained and rinsed
1 long red chilli, finely chopped
250 ml (9 fl oz/1 cup) chicken
   stock
pink salt and freshly ground
   black pepper
2–3 tablespoons roughly
   chopped flat-leaf (Italian)
   parsley leaves, plus extra,
   finely chopped, to serve
4 eggs

Heat the olive oil in a large frying pan over medium–high heat. Add the onion and stir for a couple of minutes until softened. Add the garlic and stir for another 2 minutes until fragrant.

Add the thyme, tomatoes, cannellini beans, chilli and stock to the pan and gently stir. Season with a little salt and pepper and turn the heat down to medium–low. Simmer for around 10 minutes until reduced and thickened. Stir in the parsley, taste and adjust the seasoning if necessary.

Next, make four wells in the mixture and crack an egg into each one. Season each egg with a little salt and pepper. Cover the pan with a lid (grab the lid of a large saucepan if your frying pan doesn't have one) and cook for about 8–10 minutes or until the egg whites are cooked through (no longer translucent) and the yolks are still runny.

Remove the pan from the heat and sprinkle the extra parsley over the top. Delicious served with toast or tortillas.

This is quite a filling meal, given that it has both eggs and beans, so it's perfect for weekend brunch. — Maha

DETOX SOUP

DF // RSF // V // VG // P // 945 KJ/226 CAL PER SERVE
SERVES 4

---

1 teaspoon coconut oil

4 garlic cloves, finely chopped

4 spring onions (scallions), roughly chopped, plus extra, finely sliced, to serve

1 leek, white and pale green part only, roughly chopped

2 zucchini (courgettes), roughly chopped

60 g (2¼ oz/1 cup) roughly chopped broccoli florets

4 celery stalks, roughly chopped

4 green apples, peeled and chopped

2 tablespoons ginger, peeled and roughly chopped

¼ teaspoon ground turmeric

¼ teaspoon ground coriander

1 litre (35 fl oz/4 cups) vegetable stock

pink salt and freshly ground black pepper

120 g (4¼ oz/4 cups) kale ribbons (stalks removed, leaves sliced and massaged), plus extra, to serve

1 x 400 ml (14 fl oz) tin coconut milk

Heat the coconut oil in a large saucepan over medium heat. Add the garlic, spring onion and leek and cook, stirring frequently, for 3–4 minutes until softened.

Add the zucchini, broccoli, celery and apple to the pan and sauté for around 4–6 minutes. Stir in the ginger, turmeric and coriander and cook for another 30 seconds to a minute, until fragrant. Pour in the stock and season with salt and pepper. Bring to the boil, reduce the heat to low and simmer for 5 minutes, or until the broccoli and zucchini are just tender.

Next, add the kale and coconut milk to the pan. Simmer for another 3–4 minutes until the kale is bright green and just wilted. Remove from the heat.

Puree the soup with a hand-held blender or in batches using a blender. Season with extra salt and pepper, and sprinkle with spring onion and kale (if desired).

DEVOURED-IN-SECONDS ITALIAN CHICKEN

RSF // 1614 KJ/386 CAL PER SERVE
SERVES 2

4 boneless, skinless chicken thighs, fat trimmed
2 tablespoons Italian herb seasoning
pink salt and freshly ground black pepper
2 tablespoons extra virgin olive oil
1 onion, finely diced
2 garlic cloves, finely chopped
1 yellow capsicum (pepper), diced
1 red capsicum (pepper), diced
100 g (3½ oz) Swiss brown mushrooms, sliced
1 x 400 g (14 oz) tin whole peeled tomatoes, crushed
500 ml (17 fl oz/2 cups) chicken stock
1 chicken stock cube
130 g (4¾ oz/½ cup) Greek-style yoghurt
1 teaspoon cornflour (cornstarch)
30 g (1 oz/½ cup) small basil leaves
finely grated parmesan, to serve (optional)

Season the chicken with 1 tablespoon of Italian herb seasoning mix and a good pinch of salt and pepper.

Heat 1 tablespoon of olive oil in a large frying pan over medium–high heat. Add the chicken and cook until golden brown, 3–4 minutes on each side. Remove from the pan and set aside, keeping warm.

Heat the remaining olive oil in the pan and add the onion, garlic, capsicums and mushrooms and sauté until softened, about 5 minutes. Add the tomatoes, stock, stock cube and the remaining Italian herb seasoning mix and simmer for approximately 15–20 minutes or until thickened.

Whisk together the yoghurt and cornflour in a bowl. Add to the pan and mix well. Season with salt and pepper. Return the chicken to the pan and cook until heated through.

Scatter over the basil and parmesan (if desired). We like to serve this with baby rocket, steamed basmati rice or pasta.

HEARTY BEANS AND GREENS

RSF // VG // 1374 KJ/329 CAL PER SERVE
SERVES 4

1 tablespoon ghee
1 tablespoon extra virgin olive
   oil
1 onion, diced
4 garlic cloves, crushed
4 carrots, sliced
½ large purple sweet potato,
   diced
1 tablespoon Italian dried herb
   mix
pink salt and freshly ground
   black pepper
1 litre (35 fl oz/4 cups)
   vegetable stock
2 x 400 g (14 oz) tins cannellini
   beans, drained and rinsed
60 g (2¼ oz/2 cups) leafy
   greens (we use baby kale and
   watercress sprigs)

Heat the ghee and oil in a large saucepan over medium heat. Add the onion and garlic and cook, stirring occasionally, for 3–4 minutes until they are softened. Stir in the carrot, sweet potato, Italian herb mix and a pinch of salt and pepper and cook for 2 minutes.

Add the stock and cannellini beans to the pan. Simmer for 30 minutes until the carrot and sweet potato are tender. Remove about 2 cups of beans from the pan, place in a bowl and roughly mash with a fork. (This helps to thicken up the stock.) Return to the pan and mix well. Stir in the greens and simmer until just wilted; season with salt and serve.

note

* A purple sweet potato is actually white on the outside. And the one that is purple on the outside is white inside. Confused? Don't worry, most people are. This recipe uses purple sweet potato, so look for the one that has a white skin.

I like to shell the cannellini beans as I rinse them. I think it results in a better final product but it takes an extra few minutes. Maha can't be bothered. It's not essential, just up to you. — Sally

ONE-PAN TUSCAN SALMON

RSF // 3190 KJ/763 CAL PER SERVE
SERVES 2

1 teaspoon extra virgin olive oil
2 x 120 g (4¼ oz) salmon fillets,
   skin on, pin-boned
pink salt and freshly ground
   black pepper
1 teaspoon butter
1 small onion, finely diced
6 garlic cloves, crushed
165 g (5¾ oz/ ¾ cup) sun-dried
   tomatoes (from a jar),
   drained and chopped
110 g (3¾ oz/ ½ cup) roasted
   red capsicum (pepper) (from
   a jar), drained and chopped
245 g (9 oz/1 cup) light sour
   cream
1 tablespoon cornflour
   (cornstarch)
1 tablespoon chopped flat-leaf
   (Italian) parsley leaves

Heat the oil in a large frying pan over medium–high heat. Season the salmon on both sides with salt and pepper, and sear, skin side up first, in the hot pan for 5 minutes on each side, or until cooked to your liking (we like ours just opaque). Remove from the pan and set aside.

Melt the butter in the same pan. Add the onion and garlic and fry, stirring frequently, until light golden.

Add the sun-dried tomatoes and roasted capsicum to the pan and fry for 2–3 minutes to release their flavours. Reduce the heat to low.

In a bowl, whisk together the sour cream and cornflour until smooth. Add to the pan, stirring well until the sauce has thickened.

Return the salmon to the pan, sprinkle on the parsley and spoon the sauce over each fillet. Great with steamed rice.

CHILLI LIME CHICKEN AND RICE

DF // RSF // 2462 KJ/589 CAL PER SERVE
SERVES 4

2 teaspoons Mexican chilli
   powder
2 teaspoons smoked paprika
1 teaspoon garlic salt
¼ teaspoon cayenne pepper
4 boneless, skinless chicken
   thighs, fat trimmed
1 tablespoon extra virgin
   olive oil
625 ml (21½ fl oz/2½ cups)
   chicken stock
1 lime, zested and juiced
400 g (14 oz/2 cups) basmati
   rice, rinsed until water
   runs clear

TO SERVE

2 limes, 1 juiced and 1 cut into
   wedges
chopped coriander (cilantro)
   leaves
Greek-style yoghurt (optional)

Mix together the chilli powder, smoked paprika, garlic salt and cayenne pepper in a bowl.

Season the chicken with the spice mixture, ensuring it's well coated.

Heat the olive oil in a large saucepan over medium heat. Add the chicken and cook for 3–4 minutes on each side until golden brown. Remove from the pan.

Pour the stock into the pan and scrape the base with a wooden spoon to deglaze. Stir in the lime zest and juice and add the rice.

Return the chicken to the pan and place on top of the rice. Reduce the heat to low, cover with a lid and cook for 20–25 minutes until the rice is cooked and the liquid absorbed.

To serve, squeeze over the lime juice and fluff the rice. Sprinkle on the coriander and add the lime wedges on the side with a dollop of Greek-style yoghurt (if desired).

EASY PEASY BEEF STEW

DF // RSF // 1533 KJ/367 CAL PER SERVE
SERVES 6

1 kg (2 lb 4 oz) chuck steak,
  fat trimmed and cut into
  large cubes
1 tablespoon cornflour
  (cornstarch)
2 tablespoons extra virgin
  olive oil
2 onions, roughly chopped
10 celery stalks, roughly
  chopped
6 large carrots, roughly chopped
250 ml (9 fl oz/1 cup) tomato
  juice
1 beef stock cube diluted in
  125 ml (4 fl oz/½ cup) boiling
  water
chopped parsley, to serve
  (optional)

Preheat the oven to 150°C (300°F).

Place the chuck steak and cornflour in a zip-lock bag,
seal and shake well.

Heat the olive oil in a large casserole dish over
medium–high heat. Tip in the meat and quickly sear on
all sides until well browned. Add the onion, celery and
carrot, and pan-fry for 2–3 minutes.

Pour the tomato juice and stock into the dish, cover
with the lid and pop in the oven to cook for 4 hours
until the meat is very tender. Season with salt and
pepper to taste and garnish with chopped parsley
(if desired). Great with steamed rice.

NOURISHING DETOX CHICKEN SOUP

DF // RSF // 1042 KJ/249 CAL PER SERVE
SERVES 6

2 tablespoons extra virgin
  olive oil
1 large onion, diced
1 leek, white part only, thinly
  sliced
4 garlic cloves, crushed
3 tablespoons grated ginger
280 g (10 oz/2 cups) chopped
  celery
465 g (1 lb ½ oz/3 cups) diced
  carrots
600 g (1 lb 5 oz) boneless,
  skinless chicken thighs,
  fat trimmed, each cut into
  3 pieces
2 litres (70 fl oz/8 cups) chicken
  stock
1 tablespoon apple cider vinegar
¼ teaspoon ground turmeric
½ teaspoon chilli flakes or red
  chilli paste
180 g (6½ oz/3 cups) broccoli
  florets
140 g (5 oz/1 cup) frozen peas
15 g (½ oz/½ cup) flat-leaf
  (Italian) parsley leaves
pink salt and freshly ground
  black pepper

Heat the olive oil in a very large saucepan over medium heat. Add the onion, leek, garlic, ginger and celery and stir until softened, 5–8 minutes. Add the carrot, chicken, stock, vinegar, turmeric and chilli flakes or paste, stir and bring to the boil.

Reduce the heat to low and simmer the soup for 15–20 minutes until the chicken is cooked through. Remove the chicken from the pan and set aside to cool.

Add the broccoli, peas and parsley to the pan, and cook for 3 minutes until the broccoli is tender.

In the meantime, shred the chicken and return to the soup. Taste and season with salt and pepper if required. Serve.

ONE-POT MEDITERRANEAN PRAWNS WITH FETA

RSF // 1498 KJ/358 CAL PER SERVE
SERVES 4

2 tablespoons extra virgin olive oil

2 onions, finely diced

2 garlic cloves, crushed

2 x 400 g (14 oz) tins diced tomatoes

125 ml (4 fl oz/½ cup) fish stock or white wine

1 tablespoon Italian dried herb mix

pink salt and freshly ground black pepper

55 g (2 oz/½ cup) dry breadcrumbs

65 g (2½ oz/½ cup) feta, crumbled

1 kg (2 lb 4 oz) raw prawns (shrimp), peeled and deveined

1 handful of chopped flat-leaf (Italian) parsley leaves

Preheat the oven to 200°C (400°F).

Heat the oil in a large deep-sided ovenproof frying pan over medium–high heat. Add the onion and cook, stirring, for 4 minutes until softened a bit. Add the garlic and cook for 1 minute. Tip in the tomatoes, 125 ml (4 fl oz/½ cup) of water and the stock or wine, season with the dried herb mix and salt and pepper, and bring to the boil. Reduce the heat to medium–low and simmer the sauce for about 10 minutes until thickened.

While the sauce cooks, mix the breadcrumbs and feta together with your fingertips.

Add the prawns to the sauce, then sprinkle the breadcrumb and feta mixture over the top. Transfer the pan to the oven and bake for 12–15 minutes until the prawns are cooked through and the breadcrumbs are golden. Sprinkle on the parsley and serve.

serving suggestion

✱ This dish is great with crusty bread, and for extra flavour we crumble a little more feta on top.

VEGAN MEXICAN FIESTA

DF // RSF // V // VG // 2117 KJ/506 CAL PER SERVE
SERVES 4

2 tablespoons extra virgin
olive oil
1 small red (Spanish) onion,
finely diced
4 garlic cloves, crushed
2 capsicums (peppers) (red,
green, yellow or orange—we
use 1 red and 1 green), diced
1 x 400 g (14 oz) tin black
beans, drained and rinsed
375 ml (13 fl oz/1½ cups)
vegetable stock
750 g (1 lb 10 oz/3 cups) tinned
whole peeled tomatoes
300 g (10½ oz/2 cups) frozen
corn kernels
200 g (7 oz/1 cup) black and
white quinoa, rinsed
1 tablespoon smoked paprika,
plus extra, to serve
1 teaspoon ground cumin
1 lime, juiced
50 g (1¾ oz/1 cup) coriander
(cilantro) leaves
pink salt and freshly ground
black pepper
Greek-style yoghurt, to serve
(optional)

Heat the oil in a large saucepan over medium heat. Add the onion and cook for 2–3 minutes until softened. Stir in the garlic and capsicum, and cook for 2 minutes until fragrant.

Add the black beans, stock, tomatoes, corn, quinoa, paprika and cumin to the pan. Cover with a lid, turn the heat down to low and cook for 25–30 minutes until cooked through, the liquid has reduced fully and the quinoa is fluffy. Stir in the lime juice and coriander, and season with salt and pepper. If desired, add a few dollops of Greek-style yoghurt and an extra sprinkle of smoked paprika.

CHAPTER 3

Bowls

LOVE YOUR GUTS PARFAIT BOWL

RSF // VG // 2022 KJ/484 CAL PER SERVE

SERVES 1

130 g (4¾ oz/½ cup) Greek-style yoghurt

3 tablespoons coconut kefir

1 teaspoon SWIISH WELLNESS SUPERGREEN Superfood Powder

3 tablespoons rolled (porridge) oats

80 g (2¾ oz/½ cup) blueberries

90 g (3¼ oz/½ cup) halved strawberries

3 tablespoons granola

pulp of 1 passionfruit

1 teaspoon chia seeds (optional)

drizzle of honey, to serve (optional)

Mix together the yoghurt, kefir and SUPERGREEN powder in a serving bowl. Top with the oats, berries, granola, and passionfruit pulp, and the chia seeds and honey (if having).

tip

★ We like to serve this looking pretty but mix it all up just before we eat it!

This is one gut-lovin' bowl!

HEALTHY HEALING TURMERIC PORRIDGE

DF // RSF // VG // 1399 KJ/335 CAL PER SERVE
SERVES 2

95 g (3¼ oz/1 cup) rolled
    (porridge) oats
500 ml (17 fl oz/2 cups)
    unsweetened almond milk
1 teaspoon vanilla extract or
    vanilla bean paste
½ teaspoon ground turmeric
¼ teaspoon freshly ground
    black pepper (to help
    activate the turmeric)
½ teaspoon ground cinnamon
½ banana, mashed
1 tablespoon honey, plus extra
    for drizzling

TOPPINGS (OPTIONAL)
blueberries
raspberries
sliced banana
flaked coconut
nut butter
seeds of your choice
edible flowers

Combine the oats and almond milk in a saucepan and place over medium–high heat. Bring to the boil, then immediately reduce the heat to medium–low and stir in the vanilla, turmeric, pepper and cinnamon. Cook, stirring frequently so it doesn't stick to the bottom of the pan, for a few minutes until the liquid has been absorbed.

Add the banana and honey to the porridge and stir well with a fork, ensuring the banana is evenly distributed. Cook, stirring now and then, for a further minute or two until thickened. Serve at once, topped with your favourite toppings. Drizzle with the extra honey. Enjoy!

note

★ Black pepper contains compounds which have been shown to boost the absorption of other compounds during digestion—including curcumin (the most active ingredient of turmeric). Curcumin is known for its antioxidant, anti-inflammatory and antibacterial properties.

DECADENT (YET LEAN) CHOC CHIA PUDDINGS

DF // GF // RSF // V // VG // 626 KJ/150 CAL PER SERVE

SERVES 2

250 ml (9 fl oz/1 cup)
   unsweetened almond milk
3 tablespoons black or black
   and white chia seeds
2 teaspoons cacao powder
1 tablespoon rice malt syrup

TOPPINGS (OPTIONAL)
sliced banana
berries
figs
edible flowers
cacao powder
Greek-style yoghurt

Combine all the ingredients in a bowl and stir well. Divide between two small jars or bowls, cover and refrigerate overnight. Add toppings of choice or simply enjoy!

OVERNIGHT OATS 3 WAYS

SERVES 2

1.

1. *Vanilla coconut*

DF // RSF // V // VG
1179 KJ/282 CAL PER SERVE

95 g (3¼ oz/1 cup) rolled (porridge) oats
260 g (9¼ oz/1 cup) coconut yoghurt
125 ml (4 fl oz/½ cup) coconut milk
  (carton variety)
1 teaspoon vanilla extract or vanilla
  bean paste
2 teaspoons stevia

TOPPINGS (OPTIONAL)
pulp of 1 passionfruit, pineapple wedges,
flaked coconut

Mix the oats, yoghurt, coconut milk,
vanilla and stevia in a bowl and divide
between two small mason jars. Cover
with the lids and store in the fridge
overnight.

Before serving, top with the passionfruit
pulp, pineapple wedges and coconut.

tip

★ Overnight oats will keep in the
  refrigerator for up to 2 days, though
  taste best eaten within 24 hours.

2.

3. Peanut butter

DF // GF // RSF // V // VG
2144 KJ/513 CAL PER SERVE

250 ml (9 fl oz/1 cup) unsweetened almond
  milk
95 g (3¼ oz/1 cup) rolled (porridge) oats
1 tablespoon chia seeds
3 tablespoons peanut butter, plus extra
  for topping
2 tablespoons maple syrup, plus extra
  for topping

TOPPINGS (OPTIONAL)
sliced banana, flaked almonds, peanut
butter, maple syrup

In a small bowl, combine the almond milk,
oats, chia seeds, peanut butter and maple
syrup and stir well. Divide between two
small mason jars. Cover each jar with a lid
and set in the refrigerator overnight.

Before serving, top with the banana, flaked
almonds, an extra dollop of peanut butter
and a drizzle of maple syrup.

2. Pina colada

DF // RSF // V // VG
1989 KJ/476 CAL PER SERVE

160 g (5¾ oz/1 cup) chopped pineapple
  (tinned variety in natural juice is fine, just
  drain it well), plus extra for topping
185 g (6½ oz/1 cup) chopped mango, plus
  extra for topping
250 ml (9 fl oz/1 cup) coconut milk
  (carton variety)
95 g (3¼ oz/1 cup) rolled (porridge) oats
32 g (1¼ oz/½ cup) shredded coconut
1 tablespoon chia seeds, plus extra
  for topping
1 tablespoon maple syrup

TOPPINGS (OPTIONAL)
mango wedges, pineapple, chia seeds

Combine the pineapple, mango, coconut
milk, oats, shredded coconut, chia seeds
and maple syrup in a bowl, mix well and
divide between two small mason jars.
Cover with the lids and set in the
fridge overnight.

Before serving, top with the extra
mango wedges, pineapple and
chia seeds.

QUICK AND EASY RAMEN NOODLES

DF // RSF // VG // V // 1820 KJ/435 CAL PER SERVE

SERVES 1

90 g (3¼ oz) ramen noodles
1 x 10 g (¼ oz) sachet vegan
   dashi (we use kombu shiitake
   dashi, found at specialty
   grocers and delis)
250 ml (9 fl oz/1 cup) vegetable
   stock
1 tablespoon miso paste
8–10 snow peas (mangetout),
   trimmed
45 g (1½ oz/½ cup) sliced
   shiitake mushrooms
40 g (1½ oz/½ cup) shimeji
   mushrooms (or any other
   variety)
1 large spring onion (scallion),
   finely chopped
1 teaspoon chilli and garlic
   paste (jar variety from the
   supermarket)
1 baby bok choy (pak choy),
   trimmed, sliced lengthways

TOPPINGS (OPTIONAL)
soft-boiled egg
coriander (cilantro) leaves
bean sprouts
a drizzle of sesame oil
sesame seeds
a wedge of lime
freshly sliced chilli

Cook the ramen noodles according to the packet instructions. Drain and set aside.

Next, add the dashi to 250 ml (9 fl oz/1 cup) of water and whisk with a fork until dissolved. Pour into a saucepan, add the stock and miso paste and place over medium heat. Bring to a simmer, mixing well with a wooden spoon to ensure the miso paste is fully dissolved. Taste and, if you find it too salty, add an extra 3 tablespoons of water.

Add the snow peas, mushrooms, spring onion and chilli and garlic paste to the broth and simmer for 3–4 minutes until the snow peas are tender-crisp and the mushrooms have softened a little. Stir in the bok choy and cook until just wilted.

Pop the noodles into a bowl and pour the broth and veggies over the top. Serve with the desired toppings.

SPEEDY ROASTED SWEET POTATO SOUP

RSF // VG // 1772 KJ/424 CAL PER SERVE

SERVES 4

2 large onions, roughly chopped
2 large sweet potatoes, peeled
  and roughly chopped
4–6 garlic cloves, peeled
2 tablespoons extra virgin
  olive oil
pink salt and freshly ground
  black pepper
1 litre (35 fl oz/4 cups)
  vegetable stock
1 large handful coriander
  (cilantro) or flat-leaf (Italian)
  parsley leaves
130 g (4¾ oz/½ cup) Greek-
  style yoghurt

Preheat the oven to 180°C (350°F).

Place the onion, sweet potato and garlic on a baking tray. Drizzle with the olive oil, season with salt and pepper and roast for 30 minutes until softened.

Add the roasted veggies to a stockpot and pour in the stock. Place over medium heat and bring to the boil. Simmer for 10 minutes, then turn off the heat and blend with a hand-held blender until smooth.

Reheat the soup, spoon into serving bowls and sprinkle over the coriander or parsley. Serve with the yoghurt.

I like my soup thick, but if you want yours a bit thinner, just add more stock or water. — Sally

STICKY SWEET KOREAN CHICKEN

DF // RSF // 2289 KJ/548 CAL PER SERVE
SERVES 4

600 g (1 lb 5 oz) boneless and skinless chicken thighs, fat trimmed and quartered

3 tablespoons honey

3 tablespoons Korean chilli paste (see Note)

1 tablespoon soy sauce

1 tablespoon grated ginger

2 garlic cloves, crushed

1 teaspoon sesame oil

2 x 250 g (9 oz) packets 90-second microwave basmati rice

8 baby bok choy (pak choy), halved lengthways

3 tablespoons sesame seeds

2 spring onions (scallions), thinly sliced

75 g (2¾ oz/½ cup) kimchi

In a bowl, combine the chicken with the honey, chilli paste, soy sauce, ginger, garlic and sesame oil.

Place the chicken and marinade in a frying pan over medium heat and pan-fry, turning once, for 8–10 minutes until cooked through.

While the chicken is cooking, microwave the rice according to the packet instructions. Then microwave the bok choy in 3 tablespoons of water for 5 minutes. Drain well.

Arrange the rice and bok choy on a platter and place the chicken on top, making sure you spoon on all the delicious sauce. Scatter over the sesame seeds and spring onion and serve the kimchi alongside.

note

✳ You can get Korean chilli paste (gochujang) at most Asian grocery stores. It's really inexpensive and a little goes a long way.

SWEET AND SPICY JERK EGGPLANT

DF // RSF // V // VG // 1972 KJ/472 CAL PER SERVE
SERVES 4

2 tablespoons Jamaican jerk
spice mix (available from
supermarkets or specialty
grocers)
2 tablespoons grated ginger
4 garlic cloves, grated
4 tablespoons lime juice
125 ml (4 fl oz/½ cup) soy sauce
4 tablespoons rice malt syrup
6 spring onions (scallions), finely
chopped
2 eggplants (aubergines), cut
lengthways into 1.5 cm
(⅝ inch) thick slices
1 tablespoon extra virgin olive oil
1 x 450 g (15¾ oz) packet
2½-minute microwave
long-grain rice

SAUCE
3 tablespoons sugar-free barbecue
sauce
1 lime, zested and juiced
1 tablespoon extra virgin olive oil
1 tablespoon rice malt syrup
1 teaspoon grated ginger
¼ teaspoon cayenne pepper
1 spring onion (scallion), thinly sliced
pink salt and freshly ground black
pepper

TO SERVE
25 g (1 oz/½ cup) coriander
(cilantro) or flat-leaf (Italian)
parsley leaves
2 spring onions, thinly sliced
1 lime, sliced into wedges

In a small bowl, mix together the jerk spice mix, ginger, garlic, lime juice, soy sauce, rice malt syrup and spring onion. Then brush over both sides of each eggplant slice, coating well.

Place a chargrill pan over medium–high heat and brush with olive oil. Add the eggplant in batches and cook until char marks appear, 3–5 minutes on each side.

In the meantime, microwave the rice according to the packet instructions, and mix the sauce ingredients together in a bowl.

Spoon the rice into serving bowls and top with the eggplant. Drizzle over the sauce, scatter on the coriander or parsley and spring onion and serve with the lime wedges.

For my fellow spice and chilli lovers, if you want to take this to the next level, add a sliced habanero chilli to the eggplant seasoning, then scatter over a second thinly sliced one to serve. As a lover of all things chilli, I think this is the only way to go! — Sally

GREEK ISLAND DAYS CHICKEN BOWL

RSF // 2163 KJ/517 CAL PER SERVE

SERVES 2

2 x 150 g (5½ oz) chicken
    breasts
1 red (Spanish) onion, quartered

MARINADE
1 tablespoon extra virgin
    olive oil
2 tablespoons Greek (or lemon
    and herb) seasoning
2 teaspoons lemon zest
juice of ½ a lemon
1 teaspoon rice malt syrup
    (or honey)

TZATZIKI
130 g (4¾ fl oz/½ cup)
    Greek-style yoghurt
1½ tablespoons lemon juice
2 tablespoons mint leaves, finely
    sliced, plus extra, to serve
pink salt and freshly ground
    black pepper

CHOOSE YOUR OWN
OR HAVE THEM ALL
100 g (3½ oz) feta, cubed
10 kalamata olives, pitted
110 g (3¾ oz/½ cup) roasted red
    capsicum (pepper) from a jar
150 g (5½ oz/1 cup) sweet
    cherry tomatoes, halved
1 Lebanese short cucumber,
    sliced
250 g (9 oz) packet microwave
    brown rice & quinoa
    (optional)

Preheat the oven to 200°C (400°F).

Combine all the marinade ingredients in a small bowl.
Reserve the lemon halves after you have juiced and
zested. Add the chicken and rub the marinade into the
flesh. Set aside to marinate for around 20 minutes in
the fridge.

Place the onion in a roasting dish, together with the
reserved lemon halves and season well. Add the
chicken on top, together with any remaining marinade.
Pop into the oven to roast for around 25–30 minutes or
until the chicken is cooked through and the juices run
clear (pierce the thickest part of the chicken with a
sharp knife to check).

Combine all the tzatziki ingredients in a bowl, season
well with salt and pepper and pop into the fridge until
it's time to dish up.

Once the chicken has cooked, remove from the oven
and set aside to rest.

Microwave the brown rice & quinoa according to the
packet instructions (if using) and begin to assemble the
bowl, starting with the onion. Slice the chicken, and
add to the bowl along with your choice of components.
Top with a dollop of the tzatziki and a scatter of mint
leaves, and serve immediately.

note _____

★ You can also use store-bought tzatziki.

MOUTH-WATERING MEDITERRANEAN LAMB MINCE BOWL

GF // RSF // 2191 KJ/524 CAL PER SERVE

SERVES 4

1 tablespoon pine nuts, toasted

1 tablespoon extra virgin olive oil

4 French shallots or 1 large onion, diced

3 large garlic cloves, crushed

500 g (1 lb 2 oz) lamb mince

1½ tablespoons Middle Eastern spice mix

½ teaspoon chilli flakes

3 tablespoons roughly chopped flat-leaf (Italian) parsley leaves, plus extra, to serve

3 tablespoons roughly chopped coriander (cilantro) leaves

2 x 250 g (9 oz) packet 90-second microwave basmati rice

1 teaspoon butter

1 tablespoon golden raisins (or sultanas)

200 g (7 oz) sweet red cherry tomatoes, quartered

1 large Lebanese (short) cucumber, chopped

150 g (5½ oz oz/1 cup) pickled turnip or other pickled vegetables (available from Middle Eastern grocers)

4 heaped tablespoons store-bought baba ghanoush

4 heaped tablespoons labneh

2 flatbreads, cut into quarters (optional)

Dry-fry the pine nuts in a large frying pan over medium–high heat for a few minutes until golden brown. Tip into a bowl and set aside.

Next, heat the olive oil in the same pan over medium heat. Add the shallots or onion and garlic and cook, stirring often, for 5 minutes until golden. Add the mince, spice mix and chilli flakes and continue to cook, stirring and breaking up the lumps in the mince with a wooden spoon, for around 4 minutes or until the mince is cooked through. Turn off the heat and stir in the herbs.

Microwave the rice according to the packet instructions. Add to the pine nuts in the bowl, then mix in the butter and raisins or sultanas.

Divide the rice between serving bowls. Top with the mince, tomato quarters, cucumber and pickled veggies, dollop on some baba ghanoush and labneh, and serve immediately, with the flatbreads if desired.

KOREAN BEEF BOWL

DF // RSF // 2795 KJ/669 CAL PER SERVE

SERVES 4

1 tablespoon extra virgin
  olive oil
1 large onion, thinly sliced
1 large red capsicum (pepper),
  thinly sliced
1 large yellow capsicum
  (pepper), thinly sliced
300 g (10½ oz/4 cups)
  shredded green cabbage
500 g (1 lb 2 oz) extra lean
  minced (ground) beef
  (preferably grass-fed)
100 g (3½ oz) mushrooms,
  sliced
2 spring onions (scallions), thinly
  sliced, plus extra to serve
4 garlic cloves, crushed
2 teaspoons grated ginger
2 x 250 g (9 oz) packets
  90-second microwave brown
  rice (or rice of your choice)

SAUCE
2 tablespoons honey
2 tablespoons sesame oil
3 tablespoons lime juice
2 tablespoons rice malt syrup
3 tablespoons soy sauce
1 tablespoon water

TO SERVE
1 Lebanese (short) cucumber,
  thinly sliced
4 tablespoons kimchi
1 teaspoon sesame seeds

Combine all the sauce ingredients in a bowl, mix well and set aside.

Heat the olive oil in a large frying pan over medium heat. Add the onion and cook for a couple of minutes. Stir in the capsicums and cook for 5 minutes, then add the cabbage and cook, stirring occasionally, for a further 5 minutes or so until all the veggies are softened.

Push the veggies to one side of the pan. Add the mince, mushrooms, spring onion, garlic and ginger and cook, stirring and breaking up the lumps in the mince with a wooden spoon, for a few minutes until the mince is browned. Pour in the sauce and continue to stir until the mince is cooked through, about another minute or two.

Microwave the rice according to the packet instructions, then spoon into serving bowls. Top with the mince and veggies, cucumber, kimchi, sesame seeds and extra spring onion.

CITRUS SALMON BOWL

DF // GF // RSF // P // 2635 KJ/630 CAL PER SERVE

SERVES 2

pink salt and freshly ground black
  pepper
2 x 140 g (5 oz) salmon fillets,
  pin-boned
50 g (1¾ oz/2 cups) kale ribbons
  (stalks removed, leaves sliced
  and massaged)
90 g (3¼ oz/2 cups) baby spinach
  leaves
½ avocado, cut in half
½ large ruby red grapefruit,
  peeled and sliced
1 large orange, peeled and sliced
1 blood orange, peeled and sliced
1 tablespoon extra virgin olive oil
1 x 250 g (9 oz) packet 90-second
  microwave black rice (optional)
3 tablespoons chopped coriander
  (cilantro) leaves
1 tablespoon pumpkin seeds
  (pepitas)

MARINADE
1 teaspoon extra virgin olive oil
1 teaspoon smoked paprika
1 teaspoon ground cumin
½ teaspoon cayenne pepper
½ teaspoon garlic powder
½ lime, zested

DRESSING (OPTIONAL)
3 tablespoons extra virgin olive oil
2 tablespoons blood orange juice
  (about ½ blood orange)
1 teaspoon lime juice
1 teaspoon dijon mustard
2 teaspoons rice malt syrup

Place the marinade ingredients in a bowl and mix well. Add a large pinch of salt and pepper and the salmon, then rub the marinade into the flesh. Set aside.

Start to assemble the salad by arranging the kale, spinach, avocado, grapefruit and oranges in two bowls.

If you're having the dressing, make it now by combining the olive oil, blood orange and lime juice, mustard and rice malt syrup in a jar or jug, and mixing well.

Heat the olive oil in a frying pan over medium heat. Add the salmon and pan-fry for 4 minutes, or until you can see it has cooked part way up the side of the fillet. Turn and cook the other side for 2–3 minutes, or until the salmon is cooked to your liking (we like ours just opaque).

If having, microwave the black rice according to the packet instructions while the salmon is cooking. Set aside to cool for a few minutes.

Add the rice and salmon to the bowls and sprinkle the coriander and pumpkin seeds over the top. Serve with the dressing (if having). Enjoy!

note

✳ The salad gets quite juicy with the addition of all the citrus; however, if you like it extra saucy, this dressing works beautifully.

PAPRIKA PRAWN AND AVOCADO LIME BOWL

DF // GF // RSF // 1985 KJ/475 CAL PER SERVE
SERVES 4

2 teaspoons smoked paprika
2 teaspoons ground cumin
2 garlic cloves, grated
pink salt and freshly ground
    black pepper
1 kg (2 lb 3 oz) raw prawns
    (shrimp), peeled and
    deveined with tails left on
2 tablespoons extra virgin
    olive oil
1 butter lettuce, halved, leaves
    separated
2 tomatoes, cut into wedges
1 red (Spanish) onion, thinly
    sliced
2 corn cobs, kernels sliced off
    and microwaved for 3 minutes
1 x 400 g (14 oz) tin black
    beans, drained and rinsed
1 avocado, sliced
1 jalapeno chilli, thinly sliced
25 g (1 oz/½ cup) coriander
    (cilantro) leaves
1 lime, cut into wedges

DRESSING (OPTIONAL)

125 ml (4 fl oz/½ cup) extra
    virgin olive oil
3 tablespoons red wine vinegar
½ teaspoon ground cumin
1 lime, zested and juiced
3 tablespoons rice malt syrup

Mix together the smoked paprika, cumin, garlic and ½ teaspoon each of salt and pepper. Add the prawns and toss to ensure they are well coated.

Heat the oil in a large frying pan over medium–high heat. Add the prawns and cook for 2–3 minutes until just cooked through.

While the prawns are cooking, combine the dressing ingredients in a bowl, whisk well and set aside.

Divide the lettuce, tomato, onion, corn, black beans and avocado between two bowls, then add the prawns. Drizzle on the dressing, sprinkle over the chilli and coriander and serve with the lime wedges on the side.

BERRY YUM FRO YO

GF // RSF // VG // 1380 KJ/330 CAL PER SERVE

SERVES 4

465 g (1 lb ½ oz/3 cups) frozen
blueberries, plus extra berries
to serve (optional)
520 g (1 lb 2½ oz/2 cups)
Greek-style yoghurt
3 tablespoons peanut butter
(or any nut butter)

Combine all the ingredients in a food processor and
blitz until a creamy whip forms. Freeze in an airtight
container for at least an hour. Enjoy!

CHAPTER 4

One-tray wonders

BREAKFAST BAKE

DF // GF // RSF // VG // P // 1857 KJ/444 CAL PER SERVE

SERVES 4

1 large sweet potato, peeled and grated
4 tablespoons extra virgin olive oil
2 tablespoons harissa paste
pink salt and freshly ground black pepper
1 red capsicum (pepper), diced
1 yellow capsicum (pepper), diced
1 green capsicum (pepper), diced
1 red (Spanish) onion, finely diced
400 g (14 oz/2 cups) chopped tomatoes
4 eggs

Preheat the oven to 200°C (400°F). You will need two non-stick baking trays for this recipe.

On one tray, combine the grated sweet potato with half the olive oil and half the harissa, and season with salt and pepper. Gently toss to combine. Spread the sweet potato out in a single layer.

Mix together the capsicums, onion and tomato and place on the second tray. Drizzle over the remaining olive oil and harissa. Gently mix to combine.

Place both trays in the oven and bake for 20–25 minutes until the edges of the vegetables begin to brown.

Combine on one tray the sweet potato with the other veggies and mix well. Then, with the back of a spoon, make four indents. Gently crack an egg into each well. Sprinkle over a good pinch of salt and pepper and return to the oven to bake for around 5–8 minutes, or until the whites are set and the eggs are cooked to your taste. Serve with crusty bread.

HONEY LEMON SALMON AND VEGGIES

DF // GF // RSF // 2314 KJ/553 CAL PER SERVE
SERVES 4

500 g (1 lb 2 oz) butternut
   pumpkin (squash), chopped
   into chunks
500 g (1 lb 2 oz) Brussels
   sprouts, trimmed and halved
200 g (7 oz) broccolini, trimmed
4 x 125 g (4½ oz) boneless,
   skinless salmon fillets

DRESSING
4 tablespoons honey or rice
   malt syrup
1½ lemons, zested and juiced
2 tablespoons extra virgin
   olive oil
pink salt and freshly ground
   black pepper
mint sprigs and lemon wedges,
   to serve (optional)

Preheat the oven to 220°C (425°F). Line a baking tray with baking paper or lightly grease.

Mix together the dressing ingredients in a bowl.

Place the pumpkin, Brussels sprouts, broccolini and salmon on the prepared tray. Drizzle one-quarter of the dressing over the pumpkin, another quarter over the Brussels sprouts, another quarter over the broccolini and the remaining quarter over the salmon. Roast for around 20–30 minutes, or until salmon and veggies have cooked through. Add sprigs of mint and lemon wedges as desired and serve immediately (we like to leave it on the tray!). Enjoy!

CAIRO NIGHTS CHICKPEA AND CAULIFLOWER BAKE

DF // GF // RSF // V // VG // 2516 KJ/602 CAL PER SERVE

SERVES 4

4 tablespoons extra virgin
   olive oil
4 tablespoons Middle Eastern
   spice mix
1 head of cauliflower, sliced into
   4 thick 'steaks'
1 x 400 g (14 oz) tin chickpeas
   (garbanzo beans), drained
   and rinsed
4 tablespoons flaked almonds,
   toasted
25 g (1 oz/½ cup) roughly
   chopped mint leaves

DRESSING
135 g (4¾ oz/½ cup) tahini
1 lemon, zested and juiced

Preheat the oven to 200°C (400°F). Line a baking tray with baking paper.

Combine the olive oil and spice mix in a shallow bowl. Add the cauliflower and chickpeas and gently toss to ensure they are well coated. Transfer to the prepared tray and roast for 30 minutes until cooked and golden.

To make the dressing, whisk the tahini and lemon zest and juice with 125 ml (4 fl oz/½ cup) of water in a bowl.

Sprinkle the flaked almonds and mint over the roast cauliflower and chickpeas and serve straight from the tray with the tahini dressing on the side.

I like to take the skin off my chickpeas — I think they taste better. The easiest way to do this is to give them a good rub as you rinse them. It takes a few minutes to pick the skin out but it's worth it! — Sally

MEXICAN STEAK WITH LIME MINT YOGHURT DRESSING

RSF // 2345 KJ/561 CAL PER SERVE

SERVES 2

6–8 chat potatoes, thinly sliced
2 large carrots, cut into
    matchsticks
1 tablespoon extra virgin
    olive oil
2 tablespoons Mexican
    seasoning
2 x 150 g (5½ oz) skirt steaks
    or flank

DRESSING
4 tablespoons Greek-style
    yoghurt
1 lime, zested and juiced
2 tablespoons chopped mint
    leaves, plus extra sprigs,
    to serve
pink salt and freshly ground
    black pepper

Preheat the oven to 200°C (400°F).

Toss the potato and carrot in the olive oil and half the seasoning and spread out on a baking tray, leaving room for the steak.

Press the remaining seasoning onto the steaks, making sure to coat both sides, then place on the baking tray with the veggies. Roast for 10 minutes. Remove the steak, transfer to a plate and set aside in a warm place to rest. Return the tray to the oven and bake the veggies for a further 4–5 minutes until cooked through.

While the steak and veggies are in the oven, mix together the yoghurt, lime zest and juice, mint and salt and pepper in a small bowl.

Before serving, thickly slice the steak and serve with the veggies and lime mint yoghurt dressing, garnished with sprigs of mint.

ROASTED MEXICAN KALE AND BEAN

RSF // VG // 1847 KJ/442 CAL PER SERVE

SERVES 4

120 g (4¼ oz/4 cups) kale ribbons (stalks removed, leaves sliced and massaged)
200 g (7 oz/1 cup) fresh or tinned, drained and rinsed corn kernels
1 red capsicum (pepper), finely diced
1 x 400 g (14 oz) tin pinto beans, drained and rinsed
2 tablespoons extra virgin olive oil
1 tablespoon Mexican seasoning
pink salt and freshly ground black pepper

DRESSING (OPTIONAL)

2 avocados, mashed
2 limes, zested and juiced
130 g (4¾ oz/½ cup) Greek-style yoghurt
25 g (1 oz/½ cup) finely chopped coriander (cilantro) leaves

Preheat the oven to 200°C (400°F).

Place the kale, corn, capsicum and pinto beans on a baking tray. Drizzle on the olive oil and sprinkle over the seasoning and a generous pinch of salt and pepper. Toss to ensure the vegetables are well coated. Bake for 12–15 minutes until the corn and capsicum have softened and the kale is crispy.

While the veggies are baking, make the dressing by mixing together the avocado, lime zest and juice, yoghurt and coriander in a bowl. Season with salt and pepper.

Serve the salad on the baking tray with the dressing on the side.

HOISIN-GLAZED CHICKEN WITH GREENS

DF // RSF // 2492 KJ/596 CAL PER SERVE

SERVES 4

125 ml (4 fl oz/½ cup) hoisin sauce
2 tablespoons soy sauce
12 small chicken drumsticks
2 bunches of broccolini, ends trimmed
1 tablespoon sesame oil
1 teaspoon garlic salt
1 small red chilli, thinly sliced
3 tablespoons sesame seeds (optional)
2 x 250 g (9 oz) packets 90-second microwave jasmine rice, cooked (optional)

Preheat the oven to 210°C (425°F). Line a baking tray with baking paper.

Mix together the hoisin and soy sauces in a bowl.

Cut slits into the flesh on the drumsticks, then brush on two-thirds of the sauce, ensuring that it gets into the slits and under the skin. Reserve the rest of the sauce. Spread the chicken on the prepared tray and roast for 20 minutes.

While the chicken is roasting, place the broccolini in a shallow bowl, drizzle over the sesame oil, sprinkle on the garlic salt and chilli and toss well.

Remove the tray from the oven, turn the drumsticks, brush with reserved sauce and sprinkle on the sesame seeds. Tip the broccolini onto the tray, and return to the oven for a further 10 minutes until the chicken has cooked through.

If serving with jasmine rice, microwave it just before the chicken finishes and serve all together.

ONE-TRAY CRISPY COD

DF // RSF // 2034 KJ/487 CAL PER SERVE
SERVES 4

30 g (1 oz/½ cup) panko
    breadcrumbs
1 lemon, zested
pink salt and freshly ground
    black pepper
4 x 150 g (5½ oz) Murray cod
    (or blue eye trevalla) fillets,
    skin removed, pin-boned
3 tablespoons dijon mustard
2 x 400 g (14 oz) tins cannellini
    beans, rinsed
300 g (10½ oz/2 cups) medley
    of sweet red cherry
    tomatoes, halved
200 g (7 oz/2 cups) Brussels
    sprouts, trimmed and halved
1 teaspoon cayenne pepper
4 tablespoons extra virgin
    olive oil
1 large handful of finely
    chopped flat-leaf (Italian)
    parsley leaves

Preheat the oven to 220°C (425°F).

Combine the breadcrumbs and lemon zest in a bowl
and season with ½ teaspoon each of salt and pepper.

Brush the fish fillets all over with the mustard and then
coat in the panko mixture, firmly pressing it in.

Toss together the cannellini beans, tomatoes, Brussels
sprouts, cayenne pepper and 2 tablespoons of olive oil,
season with ½ teaspoon each of salt and pepper and
spread out on a large baking tray. Place the fish on the
bed of veggies and bake until the fish is golden and
flakes easily with a fork, 10–15 minutes.

Sprinkle on the parsley, drizzle on the remaining olive
oil and add salt and pepper to taste.

CHICKPEA TACOS

DF // RSF // V // VG // 1495 KJ/358 CAL PER SERVE

SERVES 6

1 x 400 g (14 oz) tin chickpeas (garbanzo beans), drained and rinsed

1 red (Spanish) onion, thinly sliced

2 tablespoons extra virgin olive oil

1–2 teaspoons garlic salt

75 g (2¾ oz/1 cup) shredded red cabbage

200 g (7 oz) sweet red cherry tomatoes, quartered

1 large handful of roughly chopped coriander (cilantro) leaves, plus extra, to serve

1–2 teaspoons smoked paprika

6 flour or corn tortillas

100 g (3½ oz) store-bought beetroot (beet) hummus (from the dip section at the supermarket)

½ avocado, sliced

4 golden pepperoncini, sliced (sold in jars in the pickles section at the supermarket or at specialty grocers. If you can't find them, substitute jalapenos instead)

1 lime, cut into wedges.

DRESSING

1 tablespoon extra virgin olive oil

2 teaspoons red wine vinegar

2 teaspoons pomegranate molasses (optional)

pink salt and freshly ground black pepper

Preheat the oven to 180°C (350°F). Line a baking tray with baking paper.

Place the chickpeas between sheets of paper towel and set aside for 5 minutes to absorb the excess water. Remove the top sheet of paper towel and let the chickpeas air-dry for 2–3 minutes. Spread the chickpeas over two-thirds of the prepared tray, spread the onion on the other third. Drizzle on the olive oil, sprinkle over the garlic salt and toss gently to coat. Pop the tray in the oven and roast for 20–25 minutes until the chickpeas are golden and the onion has caramelised.

Make the salad by combining the cabbage, cherry tomatoes and coriander in a bowl.

Mix together the dressing ingredients and add to the salad, tossing well.

Place the roast onion on a large serving platter. Sprinkle the smoked paprika over the chickpeas and shake the tray to ensure all the chickpeas are coated. Add to the platter.

Quickly microwave the tortillas, and arrange the hummus, avocado, pepperoncini, lime and extra coriander on the platter. Serve up with the salad and let everyone assemble their own tacos—it's more fun that way!

CREAMY SPAGHETTI SQUASH WITH CHORIZO AND CHILLI

RSF // 2845 KJ/681 CAL PER SERVE

SERVES 2

1 spaghetti squash (about 1 kg/
   2 lb 4 oz)
1 onion, roughly chopped
1 sausage, sliced (we like to use
   chorizo or merguez sausage)
1 tablespoon extra virgin olive
   oil
pink salt and freshly ground
   black pepper
245 g (9 oz/1 cup) light sour
   cream
1 small red chilli, finely chopped
15 g (½ oz/½ cup) finely
   chopped flat-leaf (Italian)
   parsley

Preheat the oven to 200°C (400°F).

Halve the spaghetti squash lengthways, then scoop out the seeds and discard. Place the squash, cut side down, on a non-stick baking tray. Add the onion and sausage to the tray. Drizzle the olive oil over the onion and sprinkle with a good pinch of salt and pepper. Roast for 40–45 minutes until you can pierce the spaghetti squash with a fork, and until the sausage has cooked through. Set aside to cool slightly, then, using a fork, scrape the spaghetti-like strands out of the squash.

Transfer the spaghetti squash to a bowl, add the roasted onion, sausage and sour cream. Mix well, season with salt and pepper, and sprinkle over the chilli and parsley.

note

★ Spaghetti squash is increasingly available at greengrocers. Ask your local greengrocer to order it in if you cannot find it there.

tip

★ For a show-stopping look, scoop your spaghetti squash sausage mixture and serve it inside the empty squash 'boat'.

EASY ONE-TRAY PRAWN TACOS

DF // RSF // 2204 KJ/527 CAL PER SERVE

SERVES 4

3 capsicums (peppers) (we use
a mixture of red and yellow),
sliced

1 red (Spanish) onion, sliced

1 small red chilli, deseeded
and finely chopped

2 tablespoons extra virgin
olive oil

3 tablespoons Mexican
seasoning

pink salt

600 g (1 lb 5 oz) raw prawns
(shrimp), tails on, peeled
and deveined

1 lime, juiced, plus extra wedges,
to serve

1 tablespoon garlic salt

8 flour or corn tortillas

AVOCADO SALSA
(OPTIONAL)

2 avocados, mashed

2 limes, zested and juiced

25 g (1 oz/½ cup) chopped
coriander (cilantro) leaves,
plus extra chopped, to serve

Preheat the oven to 200°C (400°F).

Place the capsicum, onion and chilli in a bowl and add
the olive oil, seasoning and 1 teaspoon of salt. Mix well
to ensure the veggies are well coated. Spread out to
cover half a large baking tray and roast for 20 minutes
until cooked through and slightly caramelised.

While the veggies are roasting, make the salsa by
mixing together the avocado, lime zest and juice,
coriander and a pinch of salt.

Once the veggies are cooked, turn the oven setting
to grill and place the prawns on top of the veggies on
the baking tray. Squeeze the lime juice over the prawns
and sprinkle on the garlic salt. Next, add the tortillas
to the tray too. Grill for 5 minutes until the prawns
are cooked through.

Serve straight from the tray with extra coriander and
lime wedges so everyone can make their own tacos.

MIDDLE EASTERN MEATBALLS

GF // RSF // 2215 KJ/530 CAL PER SERVE

SERVES 4

1 head of cauliflower, sliced into 4 thick 'steaks'
1 tablespoon extra virgin olive oil
3 tablespoons Middle Eastern spice mix
500 g (1 lb 2 oz) minced (ground) lamb
1 onion, finely diced
1 tablespoon ghee or butter
2 garlic cloves, finely chopped
1 egg
25 g (1 oz/½ cup) mint leaves
200 g (7 oz) Tzatziki (see recipe, page 105, or use store-bought)
200 g (7 oz) store-bought beetroot (beet) hummus (from the dip section at the supermarket)

Preheat the oven to 200°C (400°F). Line a large baking tray with baking paper.

Place the cauliflower on the prepared tray, drizzle on the olive oil and sprinkle over 1 tablespoon of spice mix. Roast for 20 minutes.

While the cauliflower is roasting, mix together the mince, onion, ghee or butter, garlic, egg and the remaining spice in a bowl. Roll into 20 meatballs.

Remove the cauliflower from the oven and add the meatballs to the tray. Return the tray to the oven for 10 minutes until the meatballs are cooked through and the cauliflower is tender.

Sprinkle the mint over the meatballs and cauliflower and serve straight from the tray with the tzatziki and beetroot hummus on the side.

SPICED CINNAMON FRUIT BAKE

DF // GF // RSF // V // VG // P // 1608 KJ/385 CAL PER SERVE

SERVES 8

4 apples, sliced

4 pears, sliced

4 peaches, sliced (or if using tinned peaches, then 3 cups, drained)

640 g (1 lb 6½ oz/4 cups) chopped pineapple (or if using tinned pineapple, then 4 cups, drained)

145 g (5 oz/1 cup) dried cranberries

155 g (5½ oz/1 cup) blueberries

60 g (2¼ oz/½ cup) macadamia nuts

4 tablespoons melted coconut oil

1 tablespoon ground cinnamon, plus extra, to serve

1 teaspoon freshly grated nutmeg

4 tablespoons maple syrup or rice malt syrup

coconut yoghurt, to serve (optional)

Preheat the oven to 150°C (300°F).

Mix everything together on a non-stick baking tray and ensure the fruit is well coated in the coconut oil and spices. Bake for 1 hour until the fruit has caramelised and the nuts are crunchy. Serve sprinkled with cinnamon and with a dollop of coconut yoghurt if desired.

tip

★ The fruit will be brighter and crisper if, before cooking, you place it in a large dish and add the juice of ½ lemon, cover and leave for a few hours.

CHAPTER 5
Smoothies

SUNRISE SUNSET SMOOTHIE

DF // GF // RSF // V // VG // 1032 KJ/247 CAL PER SERVE

SERVES 2

70 g (2½ oz/½ cup) diced sweet potato
1 orange, peeled and deseeded
3 medjool dates, pitted
60 g (2¼ oz/½ cup) cauliflower florets
375 ml (13 fl oz/1½ cups) coconut milk (carton variety)
2 teaspoons tahini
1 teaspoon vanilla extract or vanilla bean paste

Place the sweet potato in a microwave-safe bowl. Add 2 tablespoons of water and microwave for 1–2 minutes until the sweet potato is soft. Set aside to cool for a few minutes.

Place the remaining ingredients in a blender and pulse to combine. Add the sweet potato and pulse again until smooth and creamy. Add toppings to taste, serve immediately and enjoy!

Toppings we've used

* 1 teaspoon coconut yoghurt swirled in a glass
* coconut flakes
* orange slices

DETOX BERRY BEET BOWL

DF // GF // RSF // V // VG // P // 1049 KJ/251 CAL PER SERVE
SERVES 1

1 cooked beetroot (beet) (63 g/
2¼ oz) (we get the vacuum-
sealed packs from the
supermarket)

80 g (2¾ oz/½ cup) chopped
pineapple (tinned variety in
natural juice is fine, just drain
it well)

250 g (9 oz/2 cups) frozen
mixed berries

45 g (1½ oz/1 cup) baby spinach
leaves

250 ml (9 fl oz/1 cup)
unsweetened almond milk

1 teaspoon SWIISH WELLNESS
Tamarind Powder

Combine all the ingredients in a blender and process until smooth and thick. Pour into a bowl and serve with your desired toppings.

toppings we've used

★ mixed berries
★ chia seeds
★ mint leaves

note

★ Tamarind is known for its many healing properties, including supporting the liver, reducing inflammation in the joints and promoting fluoride detoxification (of excess fluoride quantities in the body).

ENERGY KICKER

DF // GF // RSF // V // VG // P // 1369 KJ/328 CAL PER SERVE
SERVES 2

250 ml (9 fl oz/1 cup) coconut
water

45 g (1½ oz/1 cup) baby spinach
leaves

30 g (1 oz/1 cup) kale ribbons
(stalks removed, leaves
sliced and massaged)

250 g (9 oz/2 cups) cauliflower
florets

1 frozen banana, chopped

1 orange, peeled and deseeded

3 tablespoons mint leaves

2 teaspoons SWIISH WELLNESS
SUPERGREEN Superfood
Powder

Put all the ingredients into a blender, add 125 ml
(4 fl oz/½ cup) of water and process until smooth.
Add your toppings of choice.

Toppings we've used

★ sliced starfruit
★ puffed millet

BYE-BYE BLOAT GREEN SMOOTHIE

DF // GF // RSF // V // VG // P // 760 KJ/182 CAL PER SERVE

SERVES 2

500 ml (17 fl oz/2 cups)
  coconut water
90 g (3¼ oz/2 cups) baby
  spinach leaves
125 g (4½ oz/1 cup) cauliflower
  florets
2 celery stalks, chopped
160 g (5¾ oz/1 cup) chopped
  pineapple (tinned variety in
  natural juice is fine, just drain
  it well)
1 frozen banana, chopped
3 tablespoons mint leaves
2 teaspoons SWIISH WELLNESS
  SUPERGREEN Superfood
  Powder

Put all the ingredients into a blender and process until smooth. We garnished ours with pineapple slices, sprigs of mint and edible flowers.

GLOW-GETTER COLLAGEN BOWL

GF // RSF // 1923 KJ/460 CAL PER SERVE
SERVES 1

125 ml (4 fl oz/½ cup) unsweetened almond milk
130 g (4¾ oz/½ cup) vanilla-flavoured yoghurt
250 g (8¾ oz/2 cups) frozen raspberries
1 frozen banana, chopped
¼ avocado
2 teaspoons SWIISH WELLNESS GLOW Marine Collagen Powder

Place all the ingredients in a blender and blend until smooth. Pour into a bowl and add your desired toppings.

Toppings we've used

★ extra vanilla-flavoured yoghurt
★ frozen berries
★ walnuts

GAME SET MATCHA

DF // GF // RSF // V // VG // P // 1341 KJ/321 CAL PER SERVE

SERVES 1

250 ml (9 fl oz/1 cup) coconut
milk (carton variety)

15 g (½ oz/½ cup) kale ribbons
(stalks removed, leaves
sliced and massaged)

45 g (1½ oz/1 cup) baby spinach
leaves

1½ frozen bananas, chopped

160 g (5¾ oz/1 cup) chopped
pineapple (tinned variety in
natural juice is fine, just drain
it well)

2 teaspoons matcha powder

Put all the ingredients into a blender and process until smooth. Finish with your toppings of choice.

Toppings we've used

★ blueberries
★ sliced kiwi fruit

ANTI-INFLAMMATORY GRAPEFRUIT SMOOTHIE

GF // RSF // VG // 1653 KJ/395 CAL PER SERVE

SERVES 1

1 ruby red grapefruit, peeled and deseeded

¼ avocado

80 g (2¾ oz/½ cup) chopped pineapple (tinned variety in natural juice is fine, just drain it well)

25 g (1 oz/½ cup) baby spinach leaves

130 g (4¾ oz/½ cup) Greek-style yoghurt

1 teaspoon coconut oil

Place all the ingredients in a blender and blend until smooth. Add toppings to taste.

toppings we've used

★ grapefruit slices
★ granola
★ drizzle of honey

tip

★ Peel the grapefruit over a bowl so you don't lose any of the juice.

Bone broth smoothie

Green rocket smoothie

BONE BROTH SMOOTHIE

DF // GF // RSF // P // 1442 KJ/345 CAL PER SERVE

SERVES 1

185 g (6½ oz/1 cup) frozen
  mango pieces
90 g (3 oz/2 cups) baby spinach
  leaves
30 g (1 oz/½ cup) broccoli
  florets
2 medjool dates, pitted
62 ml (2 fl oz/¼ cup) bone broth
250 ml (9 fl oz/1 cup) regular
  vanilla almond milk

Put all the ingredients into a blender and blend until smooth. Add desired toppings.

toppings we've used

★ sliced mango
★ pumpkin seeds (pepitas)
★ kiwi fruit

GREEN ROCKET SMOOTHIE

DF // GF // RSF // V // VG // P // 886 KJ/212 CAL PER SERVE

SERVES 2

250 ml (9 fl oz/1 cup) coconut
  water
45 g (1½ oz/1 cup) baby spinach
  leaves
1 small Lebanese (short)
  cucumber, skin on
¼ avocado
1 frozen banana, chopped
45 g (1½ oz/1 cup) baby
  rocket (arugula) leaves
  or 3 tablespoons rocket
  leaves (add more if you
  want extra zing)
2 blood oranges, peeled and
  deseeded
½ lime, peeled

Put all the ingredients into a blender and process until smooth. Add your toppings of choice.

toppings we've used

★ sliced cucumber ribbons
★ pomegranate seeds

BERRY TROPICAL DELIGHT

DF // GF // RSF // V // VG // P // 1447 KJ/346 CAL PER SERVE
SERVES 1

flesh and water of 1 young
    coconut
1 frozen banana, chopped
155 g (5½ oz/1 cup) frozen
    blueberries
90 g (3¼ oz/2 cups) baby
    spinach leaves
1 teaspoon vanilla extract or
    vanilla bean paste

Place all the ingredients in a blender and process until smooth. Add your toppings of choice.

toppings we've used

★ halved strawberries
★ sliced starfruit
★ extra frozen blueberries
★ edible flowers

Apple-icious smoothie

Luscious lime slushie

LUSCIOUS LIME SLUSHIE

DF // GF // RSF // V // VG // P // 1010 KJ/242 CAL PER SERVE
SERVES 2

½ lime, deseeded, skin on
½ lemon, deseeded, skin on
250 ml (9 fl oz/1 cup) coconut
    water
270 g (9½ oz/2 cups) ice cubes
2 teaspoons stevia
2 medjool dates, pitted
135 g (4¾ oz/3 cups) baby
    spinach leaves
½ zucchini (courgette), skin on

Blend all the ingredients together until you get a slushie-like consistency. We garnished ours with a wedge of lime. Serve immediately.

APPLE-ICIOUS SMOOTHIE

DF // GF // RSF // V // VG // P // 1335 KJ/319 CAL PER SERVE
SERVES 1

2 apples, skin on, cored
90 g (3¼ oz/2 cups) baby
    spinach leaves
2 medjool dates, pitted
250 ml (9 fl oz/1 cup)
    unsweetened almond milk
70 g (2½ oz/½ cup) ice cubes

Combine all the ingredients in a blender and process until smooth. We garnished ours by dipping the rim of our glass in coconut yoghurt then shredded coconut, and adding a slice of apple. Enjoy!

BLUE MOON BOWL

DF // GF // RSF // V // VG // P // 1602 KJ/383 CAL PER SERVE
SERVES 2

260 g (9¼ oz/1 cup) coconut
yoghurt
2 frozen bananas, chopped
2 teaspoons blue spirulina
powder (see Note)
1 tablespoon coconut oil
½ teaspoon stevia

Put all the ingredients into a blender and process until smooth. Add your toppings of choice.

toppings we've used

★ halved blackberries
★ sliced dragon fruit
★ sliced star fruit
★ swirl of coconut yoghurt
★ coconut flakes
★ puffed quinoa

note

★ We like to use Blue Majik blue spirulina powder, which you can find online or at health-food stores.

Spicy mango smoothie

Kiwi coconut smoothie bowl

SPICY MANGO SMOOTHIE

DF // GF // RSF // V // VG // P // 646 KJ/155 CAL PER SERVE

SERVES 1

185 g (6½ oz/1 cup) frozen
  mango pieces
½ zucchini (courgette), skin on
45 g (1½ oz/1 cup) baby spinach
  leaves
4 tablespoons unsweetened
  almond milk
½ teaspoon stevia
1 habanero chilli, seeds removed
  (or leave the seeds if you
  dare . . . Sally does!)

Place all the ingredients in a blender and blend until
smooth. Add desired toppings.

toppings we've used

★ mango slices
★ extra chilli
★ drizzle of honey

KIWI COCONUT SMOOTHIE BOWL

DF // GF // RSF // V // VG // P // 1335 KJ/319 CAL PER SERVE

SERVES 1

90 g (3¼ oz/2 cups) baby
  spinach leaves
2 frozen kiwi fruit, peeled
1 frozen banana, chopped
250 ml (9 fl oz/1 cup) coconut
  milk (carton variety)
1 teaspoon coconut oil

Place all the ingredients in a blender and blend until
smooth. Add toppings to taste.

toppings we've used

★ kiwi fruit
★ sliced strawberries
★ chia seeds

THE M.O. SMOOTHIE

DF // GF // RSF // V // VG // P // 617 KJ/148 CAL PER SERVE

SERVES 1

1 carrot, peeled
1 apple, skin on, cored
1 celery stalk, top removed
1 tomato, top removed
pinch of chilli powder (optional)

Combine all the ingredients in a blender, add 250 ml (9 fl oz/1 cup) of water, blend and enjoy!

We used the tomato top, some chia seeds and extra celery as our garnish.

HEALING GOLDEN TURMERIC SMOOTHIE

DF // GF // RSF // V // VG // P // 1095 KJ/262 CAL PER SERVE

SERVES 1

250 ml (9 fl oz/1 cup) unsweetened almond milk
185 g (6½ oz/1 cup) frozen mango pieces
1 frozen banana, chopped
½ zucchini (courgette), skin on
½ teaspoon ground turmeric (add more if you want it stronger)

Add all the ingredients to a blender and process until smooth. We garnished ours with thinly sliced zucchini and a sprinkle of turmeric.

The M.O. smoothie

Healing golden
turmeric smoothie

ACAI SKIN GLOW BOWL

DF // GF // RSF // P // 1038 KJ/248 CAL PER SERVE
SERVES 1

1 x 100 g (3½ oz) packet frozen
    acai puree
70 g (2½ oz/1½ cups) baby
    spinach leaves
1 frozen banana, chopped
2 teaspoons SWIISH WELLNESS
    GLOW Marine Collagen
    Powder
3 tablespoons unsweetened
    almond milk, plus extra
    3 tablespoons if needed

Add the acai, spinach, banana and collagen powder to a blender and pour in the almond milk. Blend and, if required, add the extra almond milk. The less almond milk you use, the thicker the consistency of your bowl.

Add your toppings of choice.

toppings we've used

* sliced banana
* dragonfruit balls
* watermelon balls
* mixed berries
* puffed quinoa
* edible flowers
* nut butter

GREEN OATS ON-THE-GO SMOOTHIE

DF // RSF // V // VG // 1956 KJ/468 CAL PER SERVE

SERVES 2

2 frozen bananas, chopped

90 g (3¼ oz/2 cups) baby
    spinach leaves

3 tablespoons rolled (porridge)
    oats

1 tablespoon chia seeds

2 medjool dates, pitted

1 tablespoon rice malt syrup

135 g (4¾ oz/1 cup) ice cubes

3 tablespoons almond butter

250 ml (9 fl oz/1 cup)
    unsweetened almond milk

1 teaspoon ground cinnamon

Put all the ingredients into a blender and process until smooth. Add your own toppings as desired.

toppings we've used

★ a swirl of almond butter in the glass
★ sliced orange
★ ground cinnamon

PEANUT BUTTER CHOCOLATE SMOOTHIE BOWL

DF // GF // RSF // V // VG // 2438 KJ/583 CAL PER SERVE

SERVES 1

2 frozen bananas, chopped
2 tablespoons peanut butter
250 ml (9 fl oz/1 cup)
    unsweetened almond milk
3 tablespoons cacao powder
45 g (1½ oz/1 cup) baby spinach
    leaves

Place all the ingredients in a blender and blend until smooth. Add your toppings of choice.

Toppings we've used

★ peanut butter
★ raspberries
★ activated buckwheat groats
★ cacao nibs

CHAPTER 6

Snacks

COCO CHOC BALLS

DF // GF // RSF // V // VG // P // 375 KJ/90 CAL PER SERVE

MAKES 12

100 g (3½ oz/1 cup) almond
    meal
100 g (3½ oz/1 cup) medjool
    dates, pitted
2 teaspoons vanilla extract or
    vanilla bean paste
3 tablespoons cacao powder
2 tablespoons shredded coconut

Place the almond meal, dates, vanilla and cacao
powder in a food processor and pulse until well mixed.

Roll the mixture into balls.

Place the coconut in a shallow bowl, then add the balls
and roll around until covered. Pop into the fridge for
about an hour before enjoying. Keep in the fridge in an
airtight container for up to 10 days.

COOKIE PROTEIN BALLS

DF // GF // RSF // VG // 547 KJ/131 CAL PER SERVE

MAKES 12

140 g (5 oz/½ cup) peanut
    butter
4 tablespoons honey
4 tablespoons vanilla pea
    protein powder (or protein
    powder of your choice)
4 tablespoons almond meal

Mix together the peanut butter and honey in a bowl.
Add the protein powder and almond meal and mix until
well combined.

Shape the mixture into 12 balls, place in an airtight
container and chill in the fridge to set, about 2 hours.
These balls will keep in the fridge for up to 2 weeks.

Coco choc balls

Cookie protein balls

SUPER SNACKIN' TRAIL MIX

DF // RSF // V // VG // 1492 KJ/357 CAL PER SERVE

SERVES 6

450 g (1 lb) shelled frozen edamame

160 g (5¾ oz/1 cup) whole almonds

145 g (5 oz/1 cup) dried cranberries

2 tablespoons extra virgin olive oil

1 tablespoon garlic salt (if you don't have garlic salt, you can use pink salt), or more to taste

Preheat the oven to 200°C (400°F).

Let the edamame thaw for a few minutes. Meanwhile, line a baking tray with baking paper.

Spread the edamame, almonds and cranberries on the prepared tray, drizzle over the olive oil and sprinkle on the garlic salt. Mix together well (using your hands). Roast for 20 minutes until the almonds are golden and the edamame is slightly charred. Keep in an airtight container for up to 1 week.

CUCUMBER ROLLS 10 WAYS

SERVES 1

1 Lebanese (short) cucumber

Halve the cucumber lengthways and scoop out the seeds with a teaspoon to create a cavity. Mix or layer filling ingredients in each half as desired. Serve in halves or sandwich together, slice and enjoy!

1. PHILLY AND SALMON

GF // RSF

746 KJ/178 CAL PER SERVE

1 tablespoon cream cheese, 1 tablespoon diced red (Spanish) onion, 2 slices of smoked salmon

2. BLT

DF // RSF // P

890 KJ/213 CAL PER SERVE

¼ tomato, thinly sliced, 1 cos (romaine) or iceberg lettuce leaf, 2 slices of trimmed short cut bacon or turkey bacon, fried until crisp

3. RBT

DF // RSF // P

577 KJ/138 CAL PER SERVE

1 tablespoon American mustard, 2 slices of roast beef, 2 slices of turkey breast (from the deli section of the supermarket)

4. CRAN-TURK

DF // RSF

477 KJ/114 CAL PER SERVE

2 slices of turkey breast (from the deli section of the supermarket), 1 tablespoon cranberry sauce

5. DIJON CHEDDAR

RSF

1009 KJ/241 CAL PER SERVE

1 tablespoon dijonnaise, 2 slices of turkey breast (from the deli section of the supermarket), 1 slice of cheddar cheese

6. MIDDLE EASTERN

DF // GF // RSF // VG // P

491 KJ/117 CAL PER SERVE

2 tablespoons baba ghanoush, 2 tablespoons chopped kalamata olives

7. SPICY EGG

DF // GF // RSF // VG

405 KJ/97 CAL PER SERVE

1 tablespoon sriracha, 1 hard-boiled egg, chopped

8. HOT HARISSA

GF // RSF // VG

445 KJ/106 CAL PER SERVE

1 tablespoon harissa paste, 2 tablespoons labneh

9. CAPRESE

GF // RSF // VG

952 KJ/228 CAL PER SERVE

75 g (2¾ oz/½ cup) sliced cherry bocconcini , ½ tomato, sliced, 2 basil leaves, pink salt and freshly ground black pepper

10. HEY PESTO

GF // RSF // VG

610 KJ/146 CAL PER SERVE

1 tablespoon store-bought pesto, 2 tablespoons cottage cheese

note ————————————————————

★ If you are making a big batch of these you can
use all the scooped-out cucumber insides to make
the Green Rocket Smoothie on page 163.

FA-WAFFLE 5 WAYS

MAKES 4 WAFFLES

1 tablespoon extra virgin olive oil, plus
   extra for brushing
1 egg
1 onion, roughly chopped
1 x 400 g (14 oz) tin chickpeas (garbanzo
   beans), drained and rinsed
3 garlic cloves, peeled
2 teaspoons ground cumin
1 teaspoon baking powder
1 lemon, zested
15 g (½ oz/½ cup) chopped flat-leaf
   (Italian) parsley leaves
pink salt and freshly ground black pepper

Place the oil, egg, onion, chickpeas, garlic, cumin, baking powder, lemon zest, parsley and salt and pepper in a food processor. Pulse until the mixture is well combined but not completely smooth.

Heat a waffle maker and brush with a little extra olive oil. Spoon one-quarter of the mixture into the waffle maker and, following the manufacturer's instructions, cook until the fa-waffle is lightly browned. Repeat with the remaining mixture.

Serve the fa-waffle with your desired topping.

1. Egg-stra delicious

DF // RSF // VG
969 KJ/232 CAL PER SERVE

4 fried eggs, sunny side up
150g (5½ oz/1 cup) finely diced kimchi
   (store-bought is fine)
sriracha, to serve

Place an egg on each fa-waffle, top with the kimchi and drizzle with sriracha.

2. The Greek

RSF // VG
1748 KJ/418 CAL PER SERVE

1 tomato, finely diced
2 Lebanese (short) cucumbers, finely diced
1 red (Spanish) onion, finely diced
25 g (1 oz/½ cup) chopped mint leaves
200 g (7 oz) feta, crumbled
2 tablespoons extra virgin olive oil
pink salt and freshly ground black pepper

Mix all the ingredients together in a bowl and dollop onto your fa-waffle.

3.

4.

5.

3. Nights on the Nile

DF // RSF // VG
1926 KJ/461 CAL PER SERVE

125 g (4½ oz/1 cup) pitted black olives,
   finely chopped
150 g (5½ oz/1 cup) preserved lemon
   rind, finely chopped
chopped mint

TAHINI DRESSING
135 g (4¾ oz/½ cup) tahini
3 tablespoons lemon juice
1 garlic clove, crushed
½ teaspoon pink salt
3 tablespoons warm water

Whisk the tahini, lemon juice, garlic, salt
and water together until well combined.
Drizzle on the fa-waffles, then scatter the
olives, preserved lemon and mint on top.

4. Beet it

RSF // VG
1461 KJ/349 CAL PER SERVE

150 g (5½ oz/1 cup) store-bought beetroot
   (beet) hummus (from the dip section at
   the supermarket)

HARISSA YOGHURT
1 tablespoon harissa paste
260 g (9¼ oz/1 cup) Greek-style yoghurt
pink salt and freshly ground black pepper
chopped parsley

Whisk the harissa yoghurt ingredients
together. Dollop on top of the fa-waffles
with the beetroot hummus and sprinkle
some chopped parsley.

5. Zesty za'atar

RSF // VG
943 KJ/226 CAL PER SERVE

150 g (5½ oz/1 cup) labneh
2–3 yellow cherry tomatoes, halved
1 tablespoon za'atar
½ lemon, zested
chopped red chilli

Dollop the labneh on the fa-waffles, top
with cherry tomatoes then sprinkle the
za'atar, lemon zest and chilli on top.

NO-BAKE PROTEIN BARS

DF // GF // RSF // V // VG // 711 KJ/170 CAL PER SERVE
MAKES 16

140 g (5 oz/½ cup) almond butter, plus extra 2 tablespoons to spread

4 tablespoons unsweetened almond milk

90 ml (3 fl oz) maple syrup

1½ tablespoons coconut oil

85 g (3 oz/¾ cup) vanilla pea protein powder (or protein powder of your choice)

140 g (5 oz/¾ cup) coconut flour

2 tablespoons cacao powder

TOPPINGS (OPTIONAL)

chopped nuts

chia seeds

pumpkin seeds (pepitas)

cacao powder

puffed millet or quinoa

activated buckwheat nibs

shredded or flaked coconut

Line a 20 cm (8 inch) square baking tin with baking paper, cutting into the corners to fit.

Combine the almond butter, almond milk, maple syrup and coconut oil in a microwave-safe bowl and heat for 60–90 seconds until warmed through. Mix thoroughly to blend in the almond butter.

To the same bowl, add the protein powder, coconut flour and cacao powder. Mix well.

Transfer the mixture to the prepared tin and pat down to flatten.

Place in the freezer for 1 hour to set. Remove and cut into squares. They will keep in an airtight container in the fridge for a month . . . assuming you don't eat them all first!

Spread with extra almond butter and add your toppings of choice.

PAPAYA BOAT 3 WAYS

1 papaya, halved lengthways

Scoop out the papaya seeds and discard. To make your papaya boat, choose from the following options.

1. Coco berry

DF // GF // RSF // V // VG // P
1483 KJ/355 CAL PER SERVE

260 g (9¼ oz/1 cup) coconut yoghurt
3 watermelon balls
2 dragonfruit balls
125 g (4½ oz/1 cup) raspberries
3 tablespoons flaked coconut
1 teaspoon maple syrup or rice malt syrup

Fill the papaya cavities with the coconut yoghurt, then top with the watermelon, dragonfruit and raspberries. Sprinkle on the coconut and drizzle over the syrup.

2. Acai

DF // GF // RSF // V // VG // P
1528 KJ/366 CAL PER SERVE

1 x 100 g (3½ oz) packet frozen acai puree
170 ml (5½ fl oz/⅔ cup) unsweetened
   almond milk, or milk of your choice
1 frozen banana
1 kiwi fruit, sliced
30 g (1 oz/¼ cup) chopped unsalted
   macadamia nuts
2 tablespoons hemp seeds
2 tablespoons blueberries

Combine the acai, almond milk and
banana in a blender to make a smoothie.
Pulse until combined—you don't want
it too runny.

Fill the papaya cavities with the acai
smoothie and arrange the kiwi slices on
top. Finish with the macadamias, hemp
seeds and blueberries.

3. Mango chia

DF // GF // RSF // V // VG
1564 KJ/374 CAL PER SERVE

250 ml (9 fl oz/1 cup) coconut milk,
   (carton variety)
3 tablespoons chia seeds
2 tablespoons honey, maple syrup or rice
   malt syrup, plus extra, to serve (optional)
½ teaspoon vanilla extract or vanilla bean
   paste
1 mango, sliced
1 tablespoon flaked coconut
edible flowers, to decorate (optional)

Combine the coconut milk, chia seeds,
sweetener and vanilla in a jar or bowl,
mix together and leave to set overnight
in the fridge.

Fill the papaya cavities with the chia
pudding and top with the mango and
flaked coconut. Add edible flowers and
drizzle with extra sweetener of choice,
if desired.

3.

SMOKY SWEET MEDITERRANEAN DIP

DF // RSF // V // VG // 547 KJ/131 CAL PER SERVE

SERVES 6

3 large red capsicums (peppers)
or 2 jars (330 g/11½ oz/
2 cups) whole roasted
capsicums, rinsed and drained

2 tablespoons panko
breadcrumbs

1 garlic clove, peeled

2½ teaspoons lemon juice

1 tablespoon pomegranate
molasses

1½ teaspoons balsamic vinegar

½–¾ teaspoon pink salt

1½ teaspoons chilli flakes

1½ teaspoons ground cumin

2 teaspoons extra virgin olive oil

3 tablespoons roughly chopped
walnuts

parsley leaves, to serve

If you're roasting your own capsicums, preheat the oven to 220°C (425°F). Line a baking tray with baking paper.

Place the whole capsicums on the prepared tray. Roast for around 30–40 minutes, turning occasionally so that the skin on all sides becomes blistered. Pop the capsicums into a bowl, cover with plastic wrap and set aside to cool (usually around 15 minutes). Carefully peel the capsicums and discard the seeds and stem so that you're left with only the flesh.

Once you have your roasted capsicum (whether from the oven or the jar), place the capsicum and all the other ingredients in a food processor and blitz until well combined but a little chunky. Top with parsley leaves and serve with toasted pita bread or crackers.

This is such a versatile dish. I also use it as a capsicum salsa to serve with other dishes, such as dukkah-spiced lamb backstraps or pan-roasted salmon and salad. — Maha

COTTAGE CHEESE 6 WAYS

SERVES 1

Layer the cottage cheese on a plate and top with one of our delicious suggestions. Mix cottage cheese and toppings well just before eating, if desired.

1. Santorini salad

GF // RSF // VG
1154 KJ/276 CAL PER SERVE

125 g (4½ oz) cottage cheese
1 tomato, finely diced
1 Lebanese (short) cucumber, finely diced
½ red (Spanish) onion, finely diced
1 large handful mint leaves
1 teaspoon extra virgin olive oil
pink salt and freshly ground black pepper

2. Dukkah delight

GF // RSF // VG
1200 KJ/287 CAL PER SERVE

125 g (4½ oz) cottage cheese
70 g (2½ oz/½ cup) diced beetroot (beet)
1 tablespoon dukkah
1 spring onion (scallion), finely chopped
1 teaspoon extra virgin olive oil
pink salt and freshly ground black pepper

1.

2.

3.

3. Berry nuts

GF // RSF // VG
1748 KJ/418 CAL PER SERVE

125 g (4½ oz) cottage cheese
2 tablespoons unsalted pistachio kernels, chopped
1 tablespoon macadamia nuts, chopped
60 g (2¼ oz/½ cup) raspberries
pinch of ground cinnamon
drizzle of honey

4. Egg-cellent egg

GF // RSF // VG
940 KJ/225 CAL PER SERVE

125 g (4½ oz) cottage cheese
1 hard-boiled egg, chopped
1 tablespoon snipped chives
pink salt and freshly ground black pepper

5. Spice up your life

GF // RSF // VG
1020 KJ/244 CAL PER SERVE

125 g (4½ oz) cottage cheese
1 tablespoon harissa paste
3 tablespoons finely chopped mint leaves
1 teaspoon lemon zest
20 g (¾ oz/½ cup) rocket (arugula) leaves
drizzle of oil

6. Tasty tabouli

GF // RSF // VG
1871 KJ/448 CAL PER SERVE

125 g (4½ oz) cottage cheese
150 g (5½ oz/1 cup) store-bought tabouli
1 teaspoon extra virgin olive oil
pink salt and freshly ground black pepper

4.

6.

5.

LOADED SWEET POTATOES 5 WAYS

SERVES 2

1 medium sweet potato, unpeeled

Preheat the oven to 200°C (400°F). Line a baking tray with baking paper.

Cut the sweet potato in half lengthways and place, cut side down, on the prepared tray. Bake for 30–40 minutes until you can easily pierce the sweet potato the whole way through with a fork.

Carefully turn over each sweet potato half. Then, using a spoon, gently scoop out a little bit of flesh from the centre, being careful not to pierce the skin. Slightly widen the sweet potato by gently pulling it apart at the sides. The aim is to create some space for the topping.

1.

2.

1. Move to the beet

GF // RSF // VG

1558 KJ/373 CAL PER SERVE

1 x 125 g (4½ oz) packet 40-second
   microwave quinoa or brown rice & quinoa,
   cooked
4 tablespoons crumbled feta
2 cooked beetroots (beets) (125 g/4½ oz)
   (we use the vacuum-sealed variety from
   the supermarket)
3 tablespoons chopped flat-leaf (Italian)
   parsley leaves
2 spring onions (scallions), thinly sliced
2 tablespoons pitted and sliced kalamata
   olives
squeeze of lemon juice, plus extra to serve
1 teaspoon extra virgin olive oil
pink salt and freshly ground black pepper

While the sweet potato is baking, make the
salad by combining all the ingredients in a
bowl and mixing well.

Fill the sweet potato halves with the beet
mixture, then give another good squeeze
of lemon juice over the top.

2. I like to salsa

GF // RSF // VG

1695 KJ/406 CAL PER SERVE

200 g (7 oz) sweet red cherry tomatoes,
   quartered
1 spring onion (scallion), thinly sliced
½ small red (Spanish) onion, diced
3 tablespoons finely chopped coriander
   (cilantro) leaves
1 x 125 g (4½ oz) tin corn kernels, drained
   and rinsed
¼ large avocado, diced
1 tablespoon extra virgin olive oil
½ lime, juiced
pink salt and freshly ground black pepper
3 tablespoons crumbled Greek feta

While the sweet potato is baking, make
the salsa by combining all the ingredients
except the feta in a bowl and mixing
well. Taste and add more salt and pepper
if needed.

Once the sweet potato is cooked, top with
the salsa, sprinkle with the feta and serve.

3. Spicy chicken

GF // RSF

1579 KJ/378 CAL PER SERVE

3 tablespoons sour cream
2 tablespoons snipped chives
½ avocado, mashed
1 teaspoon lemon juice, or more to taste
¼ teaspoon chilli flakes, or more to taste
pink salt and freshly ground black pepper
¼ cooked, skinless chicken breast, flesh
    shredded
sriracha, to serve

Mix together the sour cream and chives
in a small bowl. In another small bowl,
combine the avocado, lemon juice and
chilli flakes and mix well. Season with
salt and pepper.

Once the sweet potato halves are cooked,
top with the chicken, followed by the
avocado mixture. Dollop on the sour cream
and chive mixture, then finish by drizzling
over the sriracha.

4. Moroccan nights

RSF // VG

1086 KJ/260 CAL PER SERVE

200 g (7 oz) tinned chickpeas (garbanzo
    beans), drained and rinsed
1 tablespoon extra virgin olive oil, plus extra
    to serve
1–2 teaspoons garlic salt
3 tablespoons Greek-style yoghurt
1 teaspoon lemon juice, plus extra to serve
1–2 teaspoons smoked paprika, plus
    ½ teaspoon extra to serve
pink salt and freshly ground black pepper
3 tablespoons baby spinach leaves

Place the chickpeas between sheets of
paper towel and set aside to absorb the
excess water, about 5 minutes. Remove
the top sheet of paper towel and let the
chickpeas air-dry for 2–3 minutes. Spread
the chickpeas over the prepared tray,
drizzle on the olive oil, sprinkle over the
garlic salt and toss gently to coat.

About 10 minutes after the sweet potato
has gone in the oven, pop in the chickpeas
and roast for 15–20 minutes until golden.

While the chickpeas and sweet potato are
roasting, mix together the yoghurt, lemon
juice and smoked paprika in a small bowl.
Season to taste.

Once the sweet potato and chickpeas are
out of the oven, line each sweet potato
'boat' with the baby spinach. Next, layer on
the chickpeas, then spoon the yoghurt over
the top. Finish with a drizzle of extra olive
oil and a squeeze of extra lemon juice.

4.

5.

5. The sweetest thing

DF // GF // RSF // V // VG // P
1663 KJ/398 CAL PER SERVE

2 tablespoons coconut, cacao and nut spread
  (available from the health-food aisle of
  the supermarket) or any nut butter you
  prefer
1 banana, sliced
155 g (5½ oz/1 cup) blueberries
150 g (5½ oz/1 cup) hulled and sliced
  strawberries
3 tablespoons shredded coconut, to serve

Spread the nut butter over the roasted
sweet potato, then top with the fruit.
Finish by sprinkling on the coconut.

3.

STUFFED MEDJOOL DATES 10 WAYS

SERVES 1

1 large medjool date, pitted

Stuff the date with the filling of your choice.

1.

1. Terrific tahini

DF // GF // RSF // V // VG // P
308 KJ/74 CAL PER SERVE

½ teaspoon tahini with ¼ teaspoon desiccated coconut

4.

2.

2. Salted caramel

DF // GF // RSF // V // VG // P
295 KJ/71 CAL PER SERVE

½ teaspoon cashew nut butter with a pinch of pink salt

3.

3. The spicy goat

GF // RSF // VG
247 KJ/59 CAL PER SERVE

½ teaspoon goat's cheese with 1 slice of jalapeno chilli (more if you like it hot)

4. Gobble gobble

DF // RSF
275 KJ/66 CAL PER SERVE

¼ slice of turkey breast (from the deli) with ¼ teaspoon cranberry sauce

6.

5.

5. Lovin' labneh

GF // RSF // VG

247 KJ/59 CAL PER SERVE

½ teaspoon labneh with 4 pomegranate seeds

6. Berry nice

GF // RSF // VG

268 KJ/64 CAL PER SERVE

½ teaspoon cream cheese with 3 blueberries

7. Nuts about you

DF // GF // RSF // V // VG // P

301 KJ/72 CAL PER SERVE

slice of apple with 1 walnut

8.

8. The prosciutto of happiness

DF // GF // RSF // P

346 KJ/83 CAL PER SERVE

½ slice of prosciutto with 1 slice of pear

9. Spicy chorizo

DF // RSF // P

359 KJ/86 CAL PER SERVE

1 slice of cooked chorizo sausage with 1–2 flat-leaf (Italian) parsley leaves

9.

10. Flip it and reverse it

GF // RSF // VG

478 KJ/114 CAL PER SERVE

½ large ripe fig stuffed with 1 sliced cherry bocconcini and 1 whole pitted medjool date. Drizzle with ½ teaspoon honey.

7.

10.

YOGHURT CHIA BLACKBERRY POTS WITH ALMONDS

GF // RSF // VG // 1981 KJ/474 CAL PER SERVE

SERVES 2

260 g (9¼ oz/1 cup) reduced fat Greek-style yoghurt
1 teaspoon vanilla extract or vanilla bean paste
1 tablespoon rice malt syrup
1 tablespoon chia seeds
130 g (4¾ oz/1 cup) fresh or frozen blackberries
1 teaspoon flaked almonds, toasted
honey or rice malt syrup, to serve (optional)

Mix together the yoghurt, vanilla, rice malt syrup and chia seeds in a bowl.

Divide the yoghurt mixture between two mason jars or bowls, cover and pop into the fridge overnight. Add the blackberries, sprinkle on the flaked almonds and drizzle honey or rice malt syrup over the top, as desired. Enjoy!

PEANUT BUTTER ICE CREAM

DF // GF // RSF // V // VG // 1816 KJ/434 CAL PER SERVE

SERVES 2

3 frozen bananas, roughly
    chopped
4 tablespoons peanut butter
1½ tablespoons cacao powder
125 ml (4 fl oz/½ cup)
    unsweetened almond milk

Combine all the ingredients in a blender and blitz until smooth. Serve immediately with the toppings of your choice.

Toppings we've used

★ cacao nibs
★ peanut butter
★ buckwheat kernels

MANGO CHILLI POPS

DF // GF // RSF // V // VG // P // 156 KJ/37 CAL PER SERVE

MAKES 12

555 g (1 lb 4 oz/3 cups) frozen
    mango pieces
2 long red chillies, sliced
1 lime, zested and juiced
375 ml (13 fl oz/1½ cups)
    coconut water

Combine all the ingredients in a blender and blend. Pour into popsicle moulds and freeze overnight.

NO-BAKE CHOCOLATE PIE

DF // RSF // V // VG // 2288 KJ/547 CAL PER SERVE

SERVES 12

BASE

240 g (8¾ oz/1½ cups) whole
   almonds
95 g (3¼ oz/1 cup) rolled
   (porridge) oats
¼ teaspoon pink salt
6 medjool dates, pitted
4 tablespoons coconut oil

FILLING

310 g (11 oz/2 cups) salted
   macadamia nuts
1 x 400 ml (14 fl oz) tin coconut
   milk
250 ml (9 fl oz/1 cup) rice malt
   syrup
4 heaped tablespoons cacao
   powder
1 teaspoon vanilla extract or
   vanilla bean paste

TOPPING (OPTIONAL)

125 g (4½ oz/1 cup) raspberries
75 g (2¾ oz/½ cup) chopped
   unsalted macadamia nuts

Line a 20 cm (8 inch) pie dish with baking paper.

To make the base, place the almonds in a food processor and process until fine crumbs form. Add the oats, salt, dates and coconut oil and process until combined. You'll know it's ready if you squeeze the mixture between your fingers and it sticks together like dough.

Press the mixture into the base and up the side of the pie dish. Using your fingers, flatten it into a pie crust.

Next, to make the filling, add the salted macadamias to the food processor and process until a nut butter forms. At first you will see ground nuts, then wet ground nuts and finally a paste. You will have to stop and scrape down the sides of the bowl a few times. Add the coconut milk, rice malt syrup, cacao powder and vanilla and process until very smooth.

Pour the filling onto the pie crust. Freeze for at least 4 hours or overnight.

To serve, top as desired with the raspberries and macadamia nuts. Allow the pie to thaw for 45–60 minutes, then slice. Even if you don't eat it all at once, slice it up and return it to the freezer. That's much easier than waiting for the whole pie to thaw.

note

★ As kids, sometimes Mum would buy a Sara Lee Bavarian cake for us as a treat. With a biscuit base and filling that was like an ice-cream-y mousse, we loved it. This is our homage in a clean version. Mum loves it too!

QUICK AND EASY DATE BALLS

DF // GF // RSF // V // VG // P // 746 KJ/178 CAL PER SERVE
MAKES ABOUT 14 BALLS

160 g (5¾ oz/1 cup) pitted
  medjool dates (around
  12 dates)
115 g (4 oz/1 cup) walnuts
100 g (3½ oz/1 cup) almond
  meal
2 teaspoons vanilla extract or
  vanilla bean paste
½ teaspoon pink salt
65 g (2½ oz/¾ cup) desiccated
  coconut
3 tablespoons chia seeds

Place the dates in a food processor and pulse until they come together into a ball. Remove and set aside. Add the walnuts, almond meal, vanilla and salt to the processor and whiz to a fine crumbly texture. Divide the date ball into 6 pieces and add back in, pulsing until all the ingredients are well combined and you have a thick crumble that is sticky enough to shape into balls.

Line a tray with baking paper. In a small bowl, combine the coconut and chia seeds and mix well to ensure the chia seeds are evenly distributed. Roll the date mixture into balls (you should get about 14) and coat in the coconut and chia mix. Place on the prepared tray, and transfer to the fridge for about an hour. Store in the fridge in an airtight container for up to a week.

ZESTY ORANGE COCONUT BALLS

DF // GF // RSF // V // VG // 544 KJ/130 CAL PER SERVE
MAKES ABOUT 16 BALLS

155 g (5½ oz/1 cup) cashew
  nuts (raw or salted and
  roasted—either is fine)
90 g (3¼ oz/1 cup) desiccated
  coconut, plus extra for
  coating
zest of 1 orange, plus extra for
  coating
½ orange, juiced (reserve the
  other ½ orange)
½ teaspoon vanilla extract
  or vanilla bean paste
1½ tablespoons maple syrup

Line a tray with baking paper.

Place all the ingredients in a food processor and blitz until you have a sticky mixture. If the mixture is too dry, juice the reserved orange and, adding a little at a time, pulse again until you get the sticky mixture needed.

Shape the mixture into balls. Place the extra desiccated coconut and orange zest in a shallow bowl, add the balls and roll around, coating well. Place on the prepared tray and transfer to the fridge to set for an hour. These balls are best enjoyed at room temperature. Store in an airtight container in the fridge for up to 4 days.

Quick and easy
date balls

Zesty orange
coconut balls

Outtakes from the photoshoot!

Nutritional chart

RECIPE	DF	GF	RSF	V	VG	P	kJ	Cal	Page
ACAI PAPAYA BOAT	✓	✓	✓	✓	✓	✓	1528	366	197
ACAI SKIN GLOW BOWL	✓	✓	✓			✓	1038	248	177
ANTI-INFLAMMATORY GRAPEFRUIT SMOOTHIE		✓	✓		✓		1653	395	160
APPLE-ICIOUS SMOOTHIE	✓	✓	✓	✓	✓	✓	1335	319	169
BEET IT FA-WAFFLE			✓		✓		1461	349	193
BERRY NICE STUFFED MEDJOOL DATES		✓	✓		✓		268	64	207
BERRY NUTS COTTAGE CHEESE		✓	✓		✓		1748	418	201
BERRY TROPICAL DELIGHT	✓	✓	✓	✓	✓	✓	1447	346	166
BERRY YUM FRO YO		✓	✓		✓		1380	330	116
BLACK RICE AND MANGO SALAD	✓		✓	✓	✓		1234	295	36
BLT CUCUMBER ROLLS	✓		✓			✓	890	213	188
BLUE MOON BOWL	✓	✓	✓	✓	✓	✓	1602	383	170
BONE BROTH SMOOTHIE	✓	✓	✓			✓	1442	345	163
BREAKFAST BAKE	✓	✓	✓		✓	✓	1857	444	120
BYE-BYE BLOAT GREEN SMOOTHIE	✓	✓	✓	✓	✓	✓	760	182	155
CAIRO NIGHTS CHICKPEA AND CAULIFLOWER BAKE	✓	✓	✓	✓	✓		2516	602	124
CAPRESE CUCUMBER ROLLS		✓	✓		✓		952	228	188
CHICKEN SHAWARMA SALAD	✓	✓	✓			✓	1996	478	39
CHICKPEA TACOS	✓		✓	✓	✓		1495	358	137
CHILLI LIME CHICKEN AND RICE	✓		✓				2462	589	76
CITRUS SALMON BOWL	✓	✓	✓			✓	2635	630	110
COCO CHOC BALLS	✓	✓	✓	✓	✓	✓	375	90	184
COCO BERRY PAPAYA BOAT	✓	✓	✓	✓	✓	✓	1483	355	196
COOKIE PROTEIN BALLS	✓	✓	✓		✓		547	131	184
CRAN-TURK CUCUMBER ROLLS	✓		✓				477	114	188
CREAMY SPAGHETTI SQUASH WITH CHORIZO AND CHILLI			✓				2845	681	138
DECADENT (YET LEAN) CHOC CHIA PUDDINGS	✓	✓	✓	✓	✓		626	150	92
DETOX BERRY BEET BOWL	✓	✓	✓	✓	✓	✓	1049	251	151
DETOX SOUP	✓		✓	✓	✓	✓	945	226	66
DEVOURED-IN-SECONDS ITALIAN CHICKEN			✓				1614	386	69

RECIPE	DF	GF	RSF	V	VG	P	kJ	Cal	Page
DIJON CHEDDAR CUCUMBER ROLLS			✓				1009	241	188
DUKKAH DELIGHT COTTAGE CHEESE		✓	✓		✓		1200	287	200
EASY ITALIAN EGGS	✓		✓				851	204	65
EASY ONE-TRAY PRAWN TACOS	✓		✓				2204	527	141
EASY PEASY BEEF STEW	✓		✓				1533	367	79
EGG-CELLENT EGG COTTAGE CHEESE		✓	✓		✓		940	225	201
EGG-STRA DELICIOUS FA-WAFFLE	✓		✓		✓		969	232	190
ENERGY KICKER	✓	✓	✓	✓	✓	✓	1369	328	152
EUROPEAN SUMMER NIGHTS SALAD			✓		✓		2219	531	46
FAST AND EASY SNAPPER WITH PEACH SALSA	✓	✓	✓			✓	1505	360	43
FLIP IT AND REVERSE IT STUFFED MEDJOOL DATES		✓	✓		✓		478	114	207
GAME SET MATCHA	✓	✓	✓	✓	✓	✓	1341	321	159
GLOW-GETTER COLLAGEN BOWL		✓	✓				1923	460	156
GOBBLE GOBBLE STUFFED MEDJOOL DATES	✓		✓				275	66	206
GREEK FA-WAFFLE, THE			✓		✓		1748	418	190
GREEK ISLAND DAYS CHICKEN BOWL			✓				2163	517	105
GREEN OATS ON-THE-GO SMOOTHIE	✓		✓	✓	✓		1956	468	178
GREEN ROCKET SMOOTHIE	✓	✓	✓	✓	✓	✓	886	212	163
HEALING GOLDEN TURMERIC SMOOTHIE	✓	✓	✓	✓	✓	✓	1095	262	174
HEALTHY HEALING TURMERIC PORRIDGE	✓		✓		✓		1399	335	91
HEARTY BEANS AND GREENS			✓		✓		1374	329	70
HEY PESTO CUCUMBER ROLLS		✓	✓		✓		610	146	188
HOISIN-GLAZED CHICKEN WITH GREENS	✓		✓				2492	596	131
HONEY LEMON SALMON AND VEGGIES	✓	✓	✓				2314	553	123
HOT HARISSA CUCUMBER ROLLS		✓	✓		✓		445	106	188
I LIKE TO SALSA LOADED SWEET POTATOES		✓	✓		✓		1695	406	203
JAMAICAN JERK CHICKEN AND HERB SLAW	✓		✓			✓	2339	560	57
KIWI COCONUT SMOOTHIE BOWL	✓	✓	✓	✓	✓	✓	1335	319	173
KOREAN BEEF BOWL	✓		✓				2795	669	109
LOVE YOUR GUTS PARFAIT BOWL			✓		✓		2022	484	88
LOVIN' LABNEH STUFFED MEDJOOL DATES		✓	✓		✓		247	59	207
LUSCIOUS LIME SLUSHIE	✓	✓	✓	✓	✓	✓	1010	242	169

RECIPE	DF	GF	RSF	V	VG	P	kJ	Cal	Page
MACA DATE SMOOTHIE	✓	✓	✓	✓	✓	✓	1643	393	26
MANGO CHIA PAPAYA BOAT	✓	✓	✓	✓	✓		1564	374	197
MANGO CHILLI POPS	✓	✓	✓	✓	✓	✓	156	37	212
MEAT-FREE MONDAY FAST FRITTATA		✓	✓		✓		1132	271	62
MEXICAN STEAK WITH LIME MINT YOGHURT DRESSING			✓				2345	561	127
MIDDLE EASTERN CUCUMBER ROLLS	✓	✓	✓		✓	✓	491	117	188
MIDDLE EASTERN LAMB CUTLETS WITH PEARL COUSCOUS TABOULI	✓		✓				2492	596	49
MIDDLE EASTERN MEATBALLS		✓	✓				2215	530	142
M.O. SMOOTHIE, THE	✓	✓	✓	✓	✓	✓	617	148	174
MOROCCAN NIGHTS LOADED SWEET POTATOES		✓		✓			1086	260	204
MOUTH-WATERING MEDITERRANEAN LAMB MINCE BOWL		✓	✓				2191	524	106
MOVE TO THE BEET LOADED SWEET POTATOES		✓	✓		✓		1558	373	203
MUMBAI NIGHTS ROAST VEGGIE SALAD	✓	✓	✓	✓	✓		1300	311	50
NIGHTS ON THE NILE FA-WAFFLE	✓		✓		✓		1926	461	193
NO-BAKE CHOCOLATE PIE	✓		✓	✓	✓		2288	547	215
NO-BAKE PROTEIN BARS	✓	✓	✓	✓	✓		711	170	194
NOURISHING DETOX CHICKEN SOUP	✓		✓				1042	249	80
NUTS ABOUT YOU STUFFED MEDJOOL DATES	✓	✓	✓	✓	✓	✓	301	72	207
ONE-PAN TUSCAN SALMON			✓				3190	763	75
ONE-POT MEDITERRANEAN PRAWNS WITH FETA			✓				1498	358	83
ONE-TRAY CRISPY COD	✓		✓				2034	487	134
PAPRIKA PRAWN AND AVOCADO LIME BOWL	✓	✓	✓				1985	475	113
PEANUT BUTTER CHOCOLATE SMOOTHIE BOWL	✓	✓	✓	✓	✓		2438	583	181
PEANUT BUTTER ICE CREAM	✓	✓	✓	✓	✓		1816	434	211
PEANUT BUTTER OVERNIGHT OATS	✓	✓	✓	✓	✓		2144	513	95
PHILLY AND SALMON CUCUMBER ROLLS		✓	✓				746	178	188
PINA COLADA OVERNIGHT OATS	✓		✓	✓	✓		1989	476	95
PRAWN, WATERMELON AND FETA SALAD		✓	✓				1042	249	58
PROSCIUTTO OF HAPPINESS STUFFED MEDJOOL DATES, THE	✓	✓	✓			✓	346	83	207
QUICK AND EASY DATE BALLS	✓	✓	✓	✓	✓	✓	746	178	218

RECIPE	DF	GF	RSF	V	VG	P	kJ	Cal	Page
QUICK AND EASY RAMEN NOODLES	✓		✓	✓	✓		1820	435	97
RBT CUCUMBER ROLLS	✓		✓			✓	577	138	188
ROASTED MEXICAN KALE AND BEAN			✓		✓		1847	442	128
SALTED CARAMEL STUFFED MEDJOOL DATES	✓	✓	✓	✓	✓	✓	295	71	206
SANTORINI SALAD COTTAGE CHEESE		✓	✓		✓		1154	276	200
SMOKY SWEET MEDITERRANEAN DIP	✓		✓	✓	✓		547	131	199
SPEEDY ROASTED SWEET POTATO SOUP			✓		✓		1772	424	98
SPEEDY, SPICY, SMOKY SALMON AND SLAW	✓		✓				2074	496	54
SPICE UP YOUR LIFE COTTAGE CHEESE		✓	✓		✓		1020	244	201
SPICED CINNAMON FRUIT BAKE	✓	✓	✓	✓	✓	✓	1608	385	145
SPICY CHICKEN LOADED SWEET POTATOES		✓	✓				1579	378	204
SPICY CHORIZO STUFFED MEDJOOL DATES	✓		✓			✓	359	86	207
SPICY EGG CUCUMBER ROLLS	✓	✓	✓		✓		405	97	188
SPICY GOAT STUFFED MEDJOOL DATES, THE		✓	✓		✓		247	59	206
SPICY MANGO SMOOTHIE	✓	✓	✓	✓	✓	✓	646	155	173
STICKY SWEET KOREAN CHICKEN	✓		✓				2289	548	101
SUMMER SUPERFOOD SALAD		✓	✓		✓		1898	454	32
SUNRISE SUNSET SMOOTHIE	✓	✓	✓	✓	✓		1032	247	148
SUPER SNACKIN' TRAIL MIX	✓		✓	✓	✓		1492	357	187
SUPERPOWERED FOUR C SALAD		✓	✓		✓		1722	412	53
SWEET AND SPICY JERK EGGPLANT	✓		✓	✓	✓		1972	472	102
SWEETEST THING LOADED SWEET POTATOES, THE	✓	✓	✓	✓	✓	✓	1663	398	205
TANDOORI CHICKEN WITH CUCUMBER YOGHURT SALAD			✓				2142	512	35
TASTY TABOULI COTTAGE CHEESE		✓	✓		✓		1871	448	201
TERRIFIC TAHINI STUFFED MEDJOOL DATES	✓	✓	✓	✓	✓	✓	308	74	206
THREE CHEERS MEXICAN CORN SALAD		✓	✓		✓		1892	453	40
VANILLA COCONUT OVERNIGHT OATS	✓		✓	✓	✓		1179	282	94
VEGAN MEXICAN FIESTA	✓		✓	✓	✓		2117	506	84
YOGHURT CHIA BLACKBERRY POTS WITH ALMONDS		✓	✓		✓		1981	474	208
ZESTY ORANGE COCONUT BALLS	✓	✓	✓	✓	✓		544	130	218
ZESTY ZA'ATAR FA-WAFFLE			✓		✓		943	226	193

Index

Thank you

To our incredible SWIISH community: to know that we are in some way playing a part in your wellness journey fills us with so much happiness and gratitude. Thank you for loving SWIISH, and supporting all we do. It thrills us to know that you love creating delicious meals from our cookbooks to enjoy yourself or share with loved ones.

To Mum and Dad and our extended families—we love you! Thank you for your love and support. They mean everything to us, and your patience (especially you, Mum!), particularly when we're on a deadline, is so appreciated.

From Sal: to Marcus, Annabelle and Elyssa—thank you for believing in me; I couldn't love you more if I tried.

From Maha: to Matthew—thank you for always being there and for your unwavering support of all that we do. I love you more than words!

To our SWIISH team—what a force to be reckoned with. We appreciate all the energy and passion that you bring every day to our shared vision of making the world a healthier and happier place.

To Claire Kingston, Courtney Lick, David Dalton, Sarah Odgers, Rob Palmer, David Morgan, Sarah Mayoh, Sarah Baker and everyone who worked with us on this book: thank you for your hard work, continued passion, commitment and belief in us. It's wonderful to work with you all. We are so appreciative.

Connect with us

We'd love for you to check in with us at SWIISH.com, and subscribe for new recipes, videos, tips, tricks, giveaways and lots more.

YOU CAN ALSO FIND US:

* On Instagram at **@swiishbysallyo**
* On Facebook at **facebook.com/swiishbysallyobermeder**

Don't forget to tag **#SWIISH** in your snaps, selfies, healthies (healthy selfies!) and share with us your favourite recipes.

CONNECT WITH SALLY OBERMEDER:

* On Instagram at **@sallyobermeder**
* On Facebook at **facebook.com/sallyobermeder**

CONNECT WITH MAHA CORBETT:

* On Instagram at **@maha_corbett**
* On Facebook at **facebook.com/officialMahaK**